DEAR MAMA

THE LIFE AND STRUGGLES

OF A SINGLE MOTHER

WRITTEN BY: BOBBY

BOSTIC

I dedicate this book to my mother and

my sister Marquise, and my brothers.

This book was written in high honor

for our eternal womb. Dear Mama...

ISBN: 9780578636719

Book Categories: Nonfiction, Parenting, Family & Relationships, Motherhood

TABLE OF CONTENTS

1   POEM: "Mama's Story"

3   CHAPTER 1: Mama's Story

23   CHAPTER 2: Teenage Years Confiscated to An Abusive Relationship

40   CHAPTER 3: Early Adulthood Years Confiscated to Another Abusive Relationship

55   CHAPTER 4: A Poor Single Mother on Welfare

75   CHAPTER 5: Back Then Everything Seemed So Unfair

90   CHAPTER 6: Being A Mother to Other People's Children

111   **CHAPTER 7:** Mama Can Act A Fool
Too

120   **CHAPTER 8:** Till Death Do Us Part

135   **CHAPTER 9:** I Brought You into This
World and I Will Take You Out

146   **POEM:** "I Brought You into This
World and I Will Take You Out"

149   **CHAPTER 10:** Husband in Custody

161   **CHAPTER 11:** Mama Doing Time
with Her Husband

168   **CHAPTER 12:** Dealing with Her
Children's Protest of Her Husband

180   **CHAPTER 13:** When A Mother
Witnesses Her Children Take the
Wrong Direction

194   **CHAPTER 14:** The Disappointment of a Mother When Kids Turn to the Streets

206   **CHAPTER 15:** She Is Only Human and She Makes Mistakes Too

224   **CHAPTER 16:** When You're Young Teenage Kids Think They Are Grown

235   **CHAPTER 17:** Reunited with Her Husband

249   **CHAPTER 18:** The Pain of a Mother When Her Children Disrespects Her

266   **CHAPTER 19:** I Can Always Depend on Mama

276   **CHAPTER 20:** The Problems of a Troubled Family

293   POEM: "The Problems of a Troubled Family"

296   CHAPTER 21: It's Not Your Fault Mama

318   POEM: "I Am Not Giving Up"

320   CHAPTER 22: In Her Own Words: "I will never give up"

385   CHAPTER 23: In Her Own Words: "A Kind Mother to Her Undeserving Kids"

489   POEM: "Ya'll Gone Miss Me When I'm Gone"

491   CHAPTER 24: Ya'll Gone Miss Me When I'm Gone

502   CHAPTER 25: Mama's Going Home

523   ESSAY ONE: "Dear Child"

539   ESSAY TWO: "Dear Mother"

550   POEM: "Mother's Day Is Every

Day"

552   FAMILY PHOTOS

555   ESSAY THREE: "Advice I Would

Give My Younger Self"

564   POSTSCRIPTS

565   AFTERWORD

575   OTHER BOOKS BY BOBBY BOSTIC

INTRODUCTION

Part of the reason this book is titled "Dear Mama" is because the last few years of me and my mother's life spent together was like a long series of letters expressing our pain, fears, hopes, and heartaches to each other in a way that is beyond words. Only the unconditional love resulting from the mystic ties of parent and child can capture the essence of love in its rawest form between a loving mother and her child.

"The measure of life is not in the number of years one lives, but the good works that one does that nothing can obliterate."

"In all things we seek to give honor to those who have given their lives in the journey and all those who lived their lives through pain and suffering in order that we might do this work today."

– Afeni Shakr

MAMA'S STORY

I present to you my mother's story
This one is full of glory
Dedicated to my eternal womb
Created, rested in an everlasting
universal tomb

She is the greatest woman I know
Daddy wasn't there so mama had to
run the show
She did do well
So now her story I tell

Before I was born, she was great
A woman destined to live her fate
She sacrificed her all for her babies
This here is a special lady

All of the wonderful things she did
Just for the sake of her kids
For us did she live
To us everything did she give

Her every struggle was for her
offspring
Us into this world did she bring
Love and mercy was her personality
Caring for her children is her first
priority

We love you mother
Signed with the signature of my sister
and both of my brothers
Unto us she gave life
For her this book I write

~Mama's Story~

Chapter 1

Awaken from a night sleep, shaking with sorrow thinking about my mother and her unconditional love for her children. Something I often ponder on, but it is hard to comprehend the mystic ties between parent and child. All I've been able to do lately is think about my mother and the way that her every waking moment was centered around the love and care of her kids.

In this chapter, I will travel back to the womb of my mother and give a brief sketch of her childhood. Her personal life in particular seemed to cease to exist when she gave birth to her children, they became her life. Since I was yet to be born when my mother was a child, I write this chapter from the recollections of the narratives that she gave me and my siblings about her childhood.

My mother, Diane "Dee Dee" Bostic, was born September 13, 1958 in St. Louis, Missouri. She is one of eleven children. She was raised by her mother Maybelle and her father William Bostic. Always a special little girl in her childhood, she was unique in her own way. As a child, she was ahead of her time. My mother was raised in a very large family. As a child, she was full of intense emotions and had thoughts deeper than her surroundings. She was very beautiful and shined in her own way. She had a very distinct style that made her stand out. In her mother's absence, her older sisters Lauretta and Shirley looked after her. My mother was not the perfect child. In fact, as she grew older, she became sort of a wild child. Throughout her childhood she into her fair share of trouble. Ever since her conception, she had a very strong love and infinity to her family. When she was young, she always wanted her brothers and sisters to stick together. There was some disunity and it hurt her to see people come between her family.

One can say that she had the typical childhood of growing up in a large black family, in an urban city of the 1960's. With 10 other siblings, she was surrounded with love. Of course, among 11 children there was a lot of bickering and quarreling going on. Therefore, sibling rivalry flourished at its highest height. Even at this young age it hurt her to see her brothers and sisters fighting amongst each other. When she did see them fighting, sometimes she would go off by herself and cry. For all of the days that she experienced heartache, at this she promised herself that when she had her family, she was going to do all that she could to get them to stick together. Her parents were having problems and separated off and on. Witnessing all of this, she desired to have a better life. There had to be better things in life outside of what she saw around her every day.

All these things combined built up in her a great desire to get away from it all. In this sense, she was not a normal child. Normally, children thrive off quarreling amongst their brothers and sisters. This is a normal tradition in the generations of all families. Most have accepted it to be natural for siblings to bicker among themselves throughout their childhood. There was just something different about this child Diane Bostic. They called her Dee-Dee.

Well, Dee-Dee never liked it when her brothers and sisters or mother and father argued with each other, especially in the presence of other people. She always felt a great sense of pain when her family quarreled, and she often wondered if they would ever truly come together as one. As a result of this, she promised herself that she would get away from this pain at the first available opportunity. She would see a change somehow and some way, even if she had to see change through the family that she planned on having on her own one day. Therefore, this became one of her earliest dreams.

Her mother and father constantly fell out and separated, and this really bothered her also. Sometimes when they separated, her mother would leave for a while. During these times, she would be under the care of her older sisters. As a child, this hurt her, and she could not understand it. Therefore, she made a promise to herself that her children would never be without her as long as she lived.

My mother was very intelligent as a child and she was a good student in school in her earlier years. But the older she got, she began to get into more trouble. Being unsatisfied with her surroundings caused her great turmoil inside and she started acting up in school. Dating was very popular among girls her age. Now at age 13, she was remarkably beautiful. At the blossoming of her youth, she had very fine physical features. She was dating at this time. It was not long before she was to meet a somewhat older man. After she caught his eye, he pursued her until he got her. Now he had a very beautiful young woman whom he could call his own. Something was holding him back from really enjoying his relationship with her, so he set his attention to this problem. His young woman still lived at home with her parents. As time went on, she shared her hopes and dreams with him, and he carried her in the signs and hopes that he would help make her dreams a reality. He convinced her that in order to do that, she must move away from home in order for him to provide a happy home for them. So, she was torn between making the decision whether or not to move away from home. This was a very difficult decision for a girl her age to be making. Looking for someone to confide in, she turned to her sister Carol. They were born a year or two apart and they were very close. They shared everything with each other. Carol and my mother had a lot in common.

These two sisters were given to adventure, so I imagine that this type of conversation was very intriguing to them. The thought of running away from home and living a life of romance excited them. It was still difficult for my mother to just walk away from home. But when she looked around her household, she saw no change in sight and she wanted something better. Would her escape to a life of romance with her boyfriend give her a chance to escape the gloom of her surroundings? This was the closest chance of escape in sight. Otherwise, she would have to wait until she was much older in order to leave home. Realistically, she had to wonder how many years this would take. The opportunity was right before her to get away from it all. So, would she take this chance? For a long time during this period, she was caught in making this decision while she was only 14 years old. Imagine a 14-year-old girl thinking about leaving home and moving in with an older man. Her boyfriend swept her off her feet and she loved him. She was happy with her relationship with him, and she figured that she would be even happier with him if she took him up on his proposition to move in with him.

Somewhere in between all of this, she got pregnant. Now 14 and in the ninth grade, she made up her mind that she was going to leave home for good. I can only imagine the things that people said about my mother for leaving home at such an early age to live with a man nearly twice her age. Even I wonder how she had the courage to do this, but I understand my mother and I know she had her reasons for doing the things she did. So, moving in with her child's father was her next move. Their relationship was great at first, but soon things changed. There was another side of this man that she did not know about. Her fairytale romance was beginning to turn into a nightmare. Her world began to turn upside down. He was physically abusing her, and she loved this man. Furthermore, she was carrying his child and she knew how important it was for him to become a father. This was one of his dreams and she vowed to be a part of the dreams of the man that she loved. So, although their relationship was rough, she hoped this load in her stomach would change all of this when she delivered their child.

This baby she was going to give birth to would be her ticket out. She figured her boyfriend would change and become the man he told her he would be, and maybe he would even become better than he was when they first met. These were the hopes that she held close to her heart and they kept her going in times of hardships. However, things turned out between her and her boyfriend, she would somehow get through it because she promised herself that when she left her parents' home, she would never look back.

With this assurance, she looked to the future with great hope. Now with her own child on the way, things had to get better. Unfortunately, things were about to get even worse. A disaster was soon to befall her that would forever leave a void in her life. Her stomach was getting very large and it was soon time for her to give birth. There were great dreams that she held for her first child. But something very tragic was on the horizon that would shatter those dreams. While giving birth, she had to face death; not her own death, but the death of her child who never lived a day to see life. Her first child was stillborn. What could this mean, her young self wondered? She was told this meant her fetus was dead when it came out of her womb. She thought to herself, this cannot be happening. She just knew that her child came out alive. She named him after his father, and the baby's name was, Tyrone Bostic. She had carried him in her stomach all these months, so someone must be lying she told herself. She never wanted to accept that her child was stillborn. A piece of her would always be missing with the loss of her child. In the meantime, life had to go on for my mother. The future looked gloomy and she had a hole in her heart weighing her down heavy. She had lost her first child even before she could spend any time with him. This was such a painful event in her life that she only talked to her kids about it. She knew she would have to tell them that they had a big brother they had never known because he died at birth. At the present time, though she had no kids to share that reality with, she lived in her own pain while searching ahead hoping for a better life.

Detailed accounts from my mother's youngest sister Linda:

Bobby, I don't remember much about your mother's childhood because I was the youngest, but Dee-Dee was a survivor. She left home at an early age, around 13 or 14 years old. She was independent. When she got her head set on something, no one could change her mind. I do know when your mom loved, she loved unconditionally, she loved hard, and she was kindhearted. When I was younger, I wanted to be just like your mom. She was so beautiful. She liked to wear Levi jeans and hush puppy shoes all the time. She wore her hair in a mushroom hairstyle.

~TEENAGE YEARS CONFINED TO AN ABUSIVE RELATIONSHIP~

Chapter 2

After her miscarriage, she became pregnant again. This time with my older brother Michael. She gave birth to him when she was 15 or 16 years old. He was born on May 19,

1974. She already had some experience with raising children because she used to watch her older sister's kids when they were working to support the family. But of course, it was different when she gave birth to her own child because he was her sole priority. She already moved away from home, but she had a strong sense of independence. On the other hand, she had no work experience and no real educational experience because she dropped out of school in the ninth grade. She lived in an apartment with my brother's father, Tyrone Jones. It was a painful relationship because he beat my mother for any reason he could think of. Whatever she did was not good enough, so he physically abused her all the time.

There were so many days that my mother would sit for hours telling me about the things that she went through in this relationship. Usually, she would be drinking beer when she told me about these stories because they were very painful memories. It built up a lot of anger and helplessness in me because of what she went through. In her narration of these stories to me, I could feel her pain behind the protective mask that she had on. These stories brought tears to my eyes, and I always vowed that no man would put his hands on my mother and get away with it. I also vowed to myself that I would never beat any woman no matter what. My mother would just look at me, take a swallow of her beer, and keep on talking. I guess this was a therapeutic way for her to deal with all the pain she went through in that relationship. I also assume that she always talked to her kids about her pain because we are a part of her. She felt there was no one in the world that she would rather share her feelings with than her kids.

My mother became pregnant again very soon. This time she gave birth to her only daughter, Marquise Bostic, born on June 1, 1975. By this time, their father had exceedingly increased beating my mother on a constant basis. She was beginning to lose herself as well as losing her mind. I never understood why my mother stayed in this relationship. I used to ask her this question. Each time she attempted to explain her reasons for staying with him, it only added more confusion to my young mind. Sometimes Tyrone would beat my mother so bad that she would seek temporary shelter at her father's or one of her sister's house. She would only resort to this when he beat her so bad that she feared for her life. My uncles would go looking for him to retaliate, but every time they did, it served no purpose because my mother would go right back to him less than a week later. He would find out where she was, apologize, and promise that he would never hit her again. She would go home with him and he would beat her up again, worse than he beat her up before she left. Not wanting to keep running to her family, she would stay with this maniac. When I was very young and she would narrate these stories to me, I was hurt. But at the same time, I felt a great sense of admiration towards my little mother because she endured all of this abuse but kept her sanity and still loved so passionately. This abusive relationship she was in with Tyrone lasted about six years. During these six years, my mother underwent the psychological trauma of living with and being in love with an egotistical, abusive, and insane boyfriend. Why did she stay with this man so long? Why did she continue to go back to him after he would lure her in with his false promises? When she tried to explain the reasons for her actions and inactions within this relationship, I was too emotional to listen. All I do know is that during the six years she was with Tyrone, there was seldom a moment of happiness that she enjoyed in life because he would attempt to beat that out of her.

For some reason, out of her four children, my mother would choose me to talk to the most about her past. I had a good ear for listening and nobody in this world could ever tell me a story better than my mother did. I would listen to her until I fell asleep, and when I woke up, she would still be at the kitchen table dealing with the scars of her past. When she used to repeat some of these stories over again, my brother and sister would sneak out of the house to go play. But my mama would keep on narrating because she knew that her son, Lil Bobby, was going to hear her out. Most of these conversations took place at the kitchen table or at my bedside. If I was sleeping and no one else was around to listen, she would wake me up and tell me to come sit with her. At times, she could not hide the pain and it was written on her face.

I don't remember her telling me anything good or special about her relationship with Tyrone. She did give him credit for trying to be a good father to my sister and brother. The entire time they were together, he kept my mother locked in the prison of this abusive relationship. He would beat her up for imagining that she was looking at another man. My mother stood about four feet and twelve inches, and he was around six feet and six inches and weighed at least a hundred more pounds than she did. Sometimes he did not want her to leave the house. He was extremely jealous and even tried to keep her from seeing her family. The only right that she had in this relationship was the right to exist. He had her trapped in the prison of this relationship that he was the architect of.

All of her teenage years were spent in captivity to this harsh relationship. In between her narration of these events, she would tell me about how love is blind. She could not get her point across to me for obvious reasons. I was a child and knew nothing of relationships and this kind of love. The other reason was because she was a different woman now and it was difficult for me to even imagine her allowing some man to take her through what Tyrone took her through. He was a petty street hustler and he did carpentry work, worked on cars, and gambled, or whatever else he had to do to support his family. She would tell me of a few stories when he had robbed people in dice games, and she would be in the car frightened. There were other incidents that went on which jeopardized their safety on a day to day basis. My memory of those particular episodes is very vague. Tyrone was involved in his street activities, while my mother was left home to take care of my brother and sister. She never knew what to expect when Tyrone came home, or if he would come home alive. She was not an angel, and she did go out and party with her sisters sometimes because she had very few friends. All her old friends were graduating from high school, while she was locked up in whatever house or apartment that she and Tyrone lived in. Even her sisters, whom she was close to, only knew that their sister left home when she was 14 years old, only to be seen when Tyrone had beat her so bad that she would go home to escape him for a couple of days.

All her teenage years were spent alienated from her family, friends, and even herself. The only life that she knew was the life of captivity to Tyrone and raising their kids, while trying to please a man that could not be pleased.

As a young man, there's nothing in my life that I can imagine experiencing that would begin to prepare me to understand how my mother underwent all of this physical, emotional, and psychological abuse at the hands of her children's father. Emerging from her late teenage years to early adulthood years, her relationship with Tyrone was becoming so unbearable that she was looking her sanity. This prompted her to open her eyes and make plans to finally leave Tyrone. It was not easy for her to leave him. It was not easy at all. Around 19 years old, she first had to escape the physical prison that he had her confined in. So, one day he left the house and she packed all of the stuff that she could carry, took her kids, and left. Of course, he searched for her all over the city. This time her brothers and her father were sure that she was not going to go back to him, so they put her under their protection, and she was safe with them as she moved into her own apartment. When she moved, she lived in fear because Tyrone was always looking for her. So, she moved from location to location, all over the city of St. Louis. Finally, she was able to leave this man and he got the message and left her alone. She was finally relieved of his abuse and she was still young. She was looking forward to the whole life

she had ahead of her.

~EARLY ADULTHOOD YEARS CONFISCATED TO ANOTHER ABUSIVE RELATIONSHIP~

Chapter 3

Off to a fresh start and free from the reigns and strains of an abusive relationship, my mother was ready to take on life. She was still young and very beautiful. After about a year or so, she met my father Bobby Payne. My father was a lady's man, and with his charm he swept my mother off her feet. She was 21 years old. My father had women all across town. My mother was soon pregnant.

I was born on January 5, 1979. It was not an easy pregnancy by far because my father was beating my mother when she was pregnant. After all that she had went through in her past relationship, she betrayed her own intelligence when my father started beating her. Somehow, she thought that his behavior patterns would change. Once again, he would beat her up and she would go to a sister's house or something, and he would sweet talk her to come back home, then beat her again. Sometimes her brothers would come to her aid, but she would go right back to my father. Eventually they started staying out of her business.

Her relationship with my father was more drastic than her relationship with Tyrone because my father was even more controlling, jealous, violent, and cruel to her. He beat her all of the time for almost anything. When she used to narrate these stories to me about my father, I could directly feel her pain, and she never tried to mask it because the pain from these stories was raw when she told them to me. The experiences that she went through in this relationship caused her to have permanent ill feelings towards my father. Still, she never stooped to the level of turning me against my father. When I used to get upset while hearing these stories and I would mutter a vengeful statement directed at my father, she always stopped me right then and there and said, "Boy I don't care what he did, he is still your father." She is a strong lady. She would tell me these stories with pain in her eyes while drinking her beer. Usually, intoxication had already set in and this is how she dealt with her pain.

My father was very jealous and controlling, so when my mother used to go out with her friends, he would wait until she got home and pick a fight with her. This was an ongoing situation that occurred in their relationship. When my mother had me, things did not really change in their relationship. As far as looks go, I came out of my mother's womb as a spitting image of my father. I look exactly like him in very detail. Nevertheless, my mother never took this out on me. She loves all of her kids equally and the same. She always told us that she had no favorite child because all of her kids were her favorite and she loved us all the same. Sometimes when my mother would be talking to me, she would say, "boy you look just like that man" referring to my father. She never mistreated me on account of that similarity. I remember one night my mother and I were up talking into the wee hours of the morning, and the radio was playing in the background and she stopped in mid-sentence and started jamming to the music. A record by this group named Heat Wave called "Always and Forever" played over the airwaves and she changed into a good mood, smiled, and said, "Boy I got pregnant with you while listening to that song." With the exceptions of a few more occasions, that was one of the rare moments that she ever told me of any good times shared between her and my father. I assume there must have been some point in their relationship that they enjoyed happiness. I guess she never told me much about those times because the bad disproportionately outweighed any good. I do not mean to paint my father as a villain in this book because today we share a tolerable relationship. But nevertheless, this is my mother's book and her story, so I must narrate the facts as I was given them from her and several other sources.

When my mother became pregnant by my father with her fourth and final child, their relationship was still rocky and very abusive. My mother got pregnant with her last child only days after she was released from the hospital after giving birth to me. My little brother Shawn was born November 1, 1979. After this pregnancy, she had a medical surgery getting her tubes tied so she could not get pregnant again. One night she told me about an occasion that took place when she was eight months pregnant with my little brother, and my father beat her real bad and pushed her down a flight of stairs. Luckily, she did not have any pregnancy complications, and my brother was born a healthy baby. I was around eight years old when she used to narrate some of these stories to me. I would just look across the table at her with astonishment because I was looking at a completely different woman than the younger version of herself who allowed these men to physically abuse her. Before I went to bed, she would console me from whatever feelings that her narration of her past had ignited in me. Nevertheless, these stories have a deep impact on me. I used to listen with great interest to her life stories. I was the child out of her four children that she spent the most time with narrating her life to. This fact is probably why I was the child who ended up writing a book about her life. As her kids, we were her favorite audience. In my mind, I can vividly go back to all of these conversations and remember the things that she told me. In a lot of instances, I know that the pain my father took her through was even worse than the trauma Tyrone took her through. Later on in life, she could at least talk to Tyrone and be around him, but on the other hand, the mention of my father raised the ire in my mother. There were Christmases and birthdays when my father used to bring me and my little brother gifts, and we would be so happy that my father brought us something and gave us some attention. Those times were rare though. All I wanted was the attention he gave us. I know my mother was upset that he was not there to support his kids. As I reflect on this, I recall that him and my mother used to engage in arguments on these rare occasions when he used to come around because he would do things to upset her like asking me such questions as, "Is she taking care of you?" These questions were more of spite to her than concern because he knew that she was taking care of us the best that she could without any support from him. If they argued, he would tell her, "I'm taking my kids with me!" She never objected because she wanted us to spend time with him. It seemed like sometimes he only did this to prevail in an argument with her because he never kept us long. He would take us around some of his girlfriends' house and they would shower him with attention by telling him how much his kids looked just like him, and they would give us stuff. I would go home so happy and brag to my mother about it. She never said anything negative, but now looking back I realize that he was not handling his responsibilities as a father. My mother raised us by herself without his assistance. Her relationship with my father was hurtful. She used to say that the only good thing that came out of that relationship was that she gave birth to me and my brother. He was another man that she tried to please who couldn't be pleased. It was not easy for her to leave him either, and after he had beat her too much, she had to go through the same things to leave him as she went through when she left Tyrone. So, she went from an abusive relationship in her early teenage years only to make the same mistake and end up in another abusive relationship in her early adulthood.

~ A POOR SINGLE MOTHER ON

WELFARE ~

Chapter 4

After finally escaping her
relationship with my father, my
mother became a poor single mother
on welfare raising four kids all by
herself. My memories of these times
are the sharpest because everything

that I write from here on out, I was old enough to witness firsthand. Seeing my own mother raise four kids by herself has caused me to appreciate the value of every single mother struggling to raise kids by themselves. I must give my mother praises where praises are due. I am sure that any son or daughter can relate to my gratitude towards the woman that brought me into this world and loved, cared, and nourished me.

Upon breaking ties with my father, she had to fend for herself alone with four young children. My mother was 23 years old at this time. The first apartment that I remember her having on her own was government sponsored section 8 low income housing in the notorious housing projects Cabanne Courts. This was one of the most violent low-income housing projects in the city of St. Louis. She refused to live with any family members, so this is where we stayed. She was determined to make it on her own without any help. The only support that she received was a monthly welfare check from the government. This check was about three-hundred-dollars and it did not even pay half of the utility bills. There was never any extra money left over and we often had to go without even basic necessities. My older brother and sister were now in school. Their clothes came from the thrift store or whatever clothes that were given to them. We would even go to the church to get free clothes from there.

Most of the time we had to go without some utility. If the gas was on, the electricity would be off. The only times that we ever had all of the utilities on was the first month that we moved into an apartment. When the bills came, we often did not have the money to pay for them, so we went without. My mother was by herself and she just did not ask for help. Like any other young woman, she went out and had fun, but her main priorities were providing for her kids. My mother had a wild side, but it never came out until after she had consumed some alcohol. While she was sober, she was the humblest, sweetest person around. But after drinking beer, she could become this little wild crazy person. Alcohol has that effect on people, especially people who are light drinkers and drink in excess of what they can tolerate. She got jobs here and there, but she never kept them too long because there was no one to watch us. We did not live in the Cabanne Courts that long. One day, my little brother was riding his big wheel and got caught in the middle of a gun battle. Soon after that, we moved. Plus, I think the landlord was complaining about us kids tearing up the interior of the apartment. She dated a few dudes, but it was nothing serious that lasted long. Most of the lowdown dudes she was meeting were not trying to help her, or they were trying to live off the little that she had. She was no fool and was on her guard about letting men get the best of her, though she fell short sometimes.

We were all still very small children, but any man that decided to hit my mother would face the wrath of all of us. We came to her defense if that happened. The next few years of her life were the hardest moments of her life. We never stayed in any apartment longer than six or eight months because we could not pay the rent. There were winters that we did not have heat and the whole family would have to sleep in one room where the kerosene heater was located. She had no boyfriends or friends that I can remember at this time. Not too many people came around. It was just her and her babies, and this is all that mattered to her anyway. The only real help that she started receiving was from my father's mother Gloria. She would bring us bags of food and clothes and stuff. She really cared. That was not her duty, but since her son fathered two of my mother's children, she felt obligated to help us out as often as she could. She would take me and Shawn to live at her house sometimes to help ease my mother's financial burden.

Times were so rough that we had to borrow electricity from our next-door neighbors. We would run an extension cord from their house to ours. At other times, we used candles and the kerosene heater as a source of light. We would use old milk jugs and other containers to get water from a neighbor's water hose. We would use this water for drinking, and at other times we would heat this water up for cooking or bathing. We never really had a phone line back then, so we were cut off from a lot of people, but we really did not have anyone to call for that matter. My older brother Mike was old enough by this time to go out and cut grass and carry grocery bags. He would do this after school and bring home about ten dollars a day, and with this money is how we got our meals sometimes. My mother would send us to the store to get the items she needed to cook us a meal.

She knew how to stretch ten dollars a long way. She always tried to make sure that we got enough to eat, but times were really hard. Mike would come in from shoveling snow sometimes, and it was cold, but he was doing his best to help his mother and younger siblings. My mother would smile and be so proud of him. There were many nights when she did not eat because it was only enough food for us kids. We used to offer her some of our food, but she would refuse it and say, "As long as my babies eat, I will be okay." During the really bad days when there was no food at all, she would fill our bellies with the hope of tomorrow. And when tomorrow came, she would find some way and go get us some food. She always made miracles. She made a way out of no way. This is my mama.

The first two weeks of the month we had food because we got free food coupons that the government gave us. The problem was that me and my siblings did not know how to balance the food and we ate everything in sight. We had big appetites. My mother would try to make the food last, but we would eat it all up. Therefore, my mama would have to go to the church pantries or relief lines to get food for us. It was not good food, but my mama was a great cook, so she would put her love into her cooking and make that food taste as best as it could. She was determined to make it on her own, and during these times we were distanced from extended family. Again, we had to move a lot because some of the apartments that we lived in were not sufficient enough for the City Housing Authority, and they said we had to move because the apartments were condemned. We had some really hard times and we made do with what we had. As I now reflect on these days, I wonder how my mother was able to undergo all of this and still keep her sanity and dignity. She is the strongest person I have ever known. The social workers from the Division of Family Services used to visit our apartments a lot, and during these times, we had to be on our best behavior and have the house clean. Before they arrived, my mother would be pacing the floor muttering things to herself while smoking a cigarette. We would continue playing and stuff, but she used to be so worried. When these people came around, she had a serious worried facial expression. Back then I did not know the significance of these visits, but now I understand that my mother could not ever let the state try to take her kids. She could not live without her kids and would do anything to keep her kids. Through whatever hard times we went through, we always stayed together. But when things seemed like they could not get any worse, they always did get worse.

Our condition was so bad that when the landlord would come for the rent money, my mother would tell one of us to go to the door and tell him that she was not there, and we had not seen her in a couple of days. We had no way to pay the rent, so a month or so later, the sheriff would serve us a summons notifying my mother that we had to move within the next 30 days. The welfare check was only about $300, and the rent was about $200. The bills were usually at least $150 each. Then we needed school clothes, toiletries, cosmetics, and other household appliances. There was no way to make it off a welfare check. Whenever my mother did find a minimum wage job that paid her about five dollars an hour, totaling about $250 every two weeks, the government would cut her welfare check in half and there was never enough money. So most of the time she only held her jobs for two weeks and quit before the government found out and tried to cut the welfare check. She could not win for losing because without education she could not make a good salary. Whenever we did get evicted from our apartments, sometimes we would see Tyrone. He used to frequent condemned apartments that one of his friends owned, and this is where he lived. He did not pay any rent or bills because he used to steal water from the city by digging up the ground and getting water like that. He also knew how to tamper with the meters and steal electricity from the utility companies. My mother was scared to do any of these things because she did not want to get caught and be taken away from her kids. However, when times got extremely bad, she would temporarily move us into one of these condemned apartments down the street from Tyrone. He did not help her financially with my brother, so it was just my mother taking care of us kids by herself. By this time, Tyrone was in his late 30s, but life had taken its toll upon him and he had a head full of grey hair. Sometimes us kids would go up to his apartment and he had a girlfriend that was nice to us, and he helped with the little that he had, but he did not have much. It was now time for me and Shawn to enroll in school, and we finally moved into a nicer apartment on Page and Hamilton Avenue. Within three months of living there, my mother met a new boyfriend named Tone. As soon as he started coming over our house, us kids hated him, and he was really ugly. We never approved of any of my mother's boyfriends, and we usually saw something wrong with all of them. But this time it was not imagination because Tone was ugly on the inside and outside. The only thing that can be said about Tone is that he did help pay some bills and added a little to our standard of living. Although we were still on welfare, we began to move up in the world. We were starting to get a taste of the normal state of life for poor folk.

~BACK THEN EVERYTHING SEEMED

SO UNFAIR~

Chapter 5

When things went wrong, somehow my mother always seemed to make it better. Nevertheless, every time something went wrong, we pointed the finger towards our mother; even though sometimes when things happened it was our fault because we were being bad children. When the welfare check came, we felt like we were rich even if it was just for that day. But as far back as my mind can remember, that welfare check could not pay all the bills. My mother only gave the companies about 50% of what was owed because that was enough for them not to cut off our electric, water, or gas off. The landlord only got about half or a third of his rent money, and she would tell him that was all the money that she had, and that she would pay him the rest. But I think these landlords always knew that was all the money they would get. Part of the problem was us kids tearing up the apartments that we moved in. We would be so loud and stuff that sometimes we were the cause of us getting put out of an apartment or house. But my mother never blamed us. She would just argue with the landlord or neighbors and come to our defense. All she would say was that, "It will be okay because mama will figure something out." Her first instinct was to protect her children at all cost. When school would start every year, we did not have new clothes like the other kids. We had to share the same old clothes that we had last year, or the clothes that we got from other people. We never had a washer and dryer, so we went to the laundromat with some of the welfare check. We were used to being poor, but it seemed so unfair. We used to get mocked by our classmates because of our clothes and shoes. I got in trouble at school a lot for fighting people who would talk about me. Then I would act bad to keep attention off my hand-me-down clothes, and I would be the best jokester in the class so other jokesters would not make fun of how poor I was. We knew many other families that were on welfare, but they were not doing as bad as our family was.

As kids, somehow, we thought that the $300 welfare check was a lot of money. When we went to the check cashing place, it sure looked like a lot of money. As I said before, us kids thought we were rich. We never had anything and that is why it seemed like a lot of money to us kids. We received a five-dollar allowance and we were so happy. One of us kids would go with her wherever she went so we could keep up with what we considered as our money. From the time that I learned how to count money, my mother always made it clear to us that the welfare check was our money. In the ghetto, everyone knew when it was welfare day. It was like a holiday in the ghetto; a time to celebrate. Everywhere went through my mother would proclaim to the spendthrifts that this was, "my babies' money." Of course, she usually drank some beer during the first week of every month. During these times, she made sure that she kept one of her kids with her, and after she purchased her six pack of beer, she would give us all her money. It would be the whole welfare check and whatever other money she had. She instructed us long ago to never give her that money no matter how many times she asked for it when she was drunk. Refusing to give her the money was not as easy as it sounds, but we never gave her the money. We would sometimes find ourselves visiting someone's house across town and these people lived in the same conditions that we did.

After my mother drank about four cans of beer, she would become a different person. Everyone knew to stay out of her way when she was drinking. But us kids knew how to handle and deal with her because she is our mama. Although she was small, when she drank beer, she would become this powerful windstorm that reached out and touched everything in its path. Usually when she would drink, she would stay up about two days and she would only sober up when she fell asleep or got arrested for disturbing the peace. When she was at home drinking, she would repeat some stories of the past that we had already heard, but she would sit one of us down and make us listen anyway. I was usually the one sitting right there and listening to her. All of our friends liked, respected, and admired my mother. They really enjoyed being over at our house around her. When we were over at their house, they would want to go over to our house to talk to my mother. They looked to her as a second mother. If there was anything that she could give or help them with, she would sacrifice it with no hesitation. This was just the way of her heart. Even though we were poor and really had nothing, my mother was still always giving something to someone else that was less fortunate than we were. Her new boyfriend was still in the picture, and in fact, his presence messed our whole family picture up. All of us kids really disliked this dude because he was very abusive towards us. As I said earlier, us kids disliked every boyfriend that my mother ever brought around us in the long term, but we really despised this dude, and we had valid reasons for this. Usually we succeeded in three or four months getting rid of all her other boyfriends. We broke them down and ran them away. But for some reason, we could not get rid of Tone. My mother had a rule with any man she that got involved with. That rule was that he had to accept her kids because we came along with her if he wanted to be with her. But we detested the fact that Tone was getting all our mother's attention. When she did not have a boyfriend, we all would go pile up in her bed and have a good time and make a mess. In fact, her bed was the family base of operation and headquarters. This routine changed when she got a boyfriend because he would want to lay up in her bed. So, we went full court press trying to get rid of Tone, but he would not leave. The longer he stayed with my mother, the uglier he got to us. It seemed like he had total domination in our household. He tried to act like he was king of our household. When we would walk into my mother's bedroom, he would be laying up like he was a king or something and for that he had to go.

This dude used to whoop us also. My mother allowed this because she needed some help with us. But I think this dude got a kick out of whipping someone else's kids. He just wasn't right, and we never considered him as a stepfather. To us he was just a bum that my mother was in a relationship with. My mother was in her early thirties and she was still beautiful like a teenager, so she could have gotten another man. Before she met Tone, we successfully ran her other boyfriends away. If I was walking down the street with her and a man started staring at her too long, I would ask him what he was looking at and tell him to quit looking at my mama. These men were naïve enough to believe that they could handle us four kids. They would measure whichever one of us that were with her at the time, and say, "You kids cannot be that bad." She would tell him, "You must not know my children, and do not let this one here fool you by himself." They would tell my mother that no kids could keep them away from her. But, after we decided that we did not like them, they did not last longer than two months. Not so with Tone. He was cruel. We assumed that eventually we would somehow get rid of him. We felt like she was putting him before us. At first, she used to make decisions with us; now he was calling the shots. This really irritated us. He was a dictator in our household. Instead of enjoying ourselves as kids, we were dreaming up ways to somehow get rid of him. Back then everything seemed so unfair.

~ BEING A MOTHER TO OTHER PEOPLE'S CHILDREN ~

Chapter 6

Going into the third or fourth year of my mother's relationship with Tone, us kids finally began to deal with the fact that they might stay together. We assured ourselves that one day they would break up, and that is the only inner relief that we received from that ordeal. Tone was an oppressor to us. During the few times that him and my mother would argue and get into fights, it was our time to retaliate. She would give us the signal and we would rush like a lion after its prey. He already knew the consequences, but he would lose his cool and leave the opportunity open for us to avenge our anger on him. We would fight him with everything in us. He would come back after a few days though, and him and my mother would make up. We hated this. When he came back, he would be back in control, and the whippings and punishments would be worse than before he left.

He would put us on punishment for any rule or regulation that we broke in the house. When we were younger, he used to make me and Shawn stand in the corner for hours as a form of punishment. Making his authority established was his main concern as far as us kids were concerned. He chastised us more than my mother ever did. He was a tyrant. I thought that my mother would never break up with him. All of our friends and family disliked him as well. On the contrary, all of his family and friends admired and respected my mother. Sometimes it would be peaceful

By the fourth year of their relationship, we moved into one of the first houses that we ever lived in. We were still having hard times back then, but it was not as bad as before. The bills stayed paid and Tone offered some financial support. I guess you could say that my mother loved him. Although the house was not owned, my mother was proud that she could move her kids into a house for the first time. My mother and sister lived in the upstairs bedrooms, and me and my brothers lived in the basement. My mother was a very kind lady, and she always let someone who did not have anywhere to go, live with us. One such person was this lady named Renee who lived with us a few years. We met her somewhere that we lived, and she became a apart of the family and lived with us a few places we stayed. My mother treated her like a daughter, and she had the same rights that we had. Renee, like many of my sister's other friends, was sort of adopted by my mother, but without the paperwork. She always showed sympathy for their plight. She only gave birth to four children, but she was a mother to a lot of other kids whose mothers were not there for them. A lot of friends' mothers were drug addicts or just did not care about their kids, and we would bring them over to our house to play and they never wanted to go home. My mother would meet them and question them about their living conditions at home, and she automatically decided to help them. She would go over to their parent's house to see their conditions for herself, and after her personal inspections, she would talk to their parents and convince them to allow their kids to move in with us. So, we always had an extra brother or sister around. They were treated like her own kids, and she gave them whatever she gave us. Sometimes her biological kids would get jealous because she was giving them a lot of attention. Tone was already in the way. But when these kids did something, Tone never tried to whip them or put them on punishment. My mother would just talk to them and tell them all that she was sacrificing for them, and they would usually straighten up. She had a special way with everyone's kids. There would be some occasions when we would be complaining about our home situation, and our friends would be telling us how blessed we were to have a mother like Dee-Dee. My mother looked very young for her age, so she had no trouble blending in with us, but she was still old fashioned to us, although she stayed fashionable. My sister was in the fifth grade now, and she was already taller than my mother. Our friends liked my mother and liked to be around her. Tone of course disliked this, but my mother did not care about that. She just liked to make us happy when she could, as well as our friends. She became the mother to our friends who did not have a mother around. My mother did not get any financial support for taking care of these kids. She did not adopt them the traditional way with .all the paperwork and stuff. Back then, things were much looser. But my mother took care of them with the little money she was able to get from her little jobs and our welfare check. Their parents did not give my mother any money to support their kids, and she got no government assistance to take care of them. She just did it out of the goodness of her heart. When they got put out of school, my mother would take them back to school. When they got sick, my mother took them to the hospital. She did whatever she needed to do for them as a mother. Over the years, her boyfriends and family used to scold her, telling her that she should send those kids back home or to a foster home. Tone went so far as to tell her that either those kids would leave, or he would leave. My mother would tell him to go ahead about his business because she would never put them kids out with nowhere to go. So, they would start arguing in front of our adopted friend, and they would be afraid that they would have to go. But my mama would tell Tone, "There goes the door, pack your stuff and leave because my kid's friends is not going anywhere. Somebody got to take care of them kids, and I promised that I would, and as long as I got a roof over my head, they can stay with me." So, after a while, they were assured of their position in our household. My mother never let them down and she never abandoned them. They were just like her kids. My mama had a lot of love in her.

Although our family was poor, my mother would always tell people, "I may not have many material things, but my kids will never need for love." When we had nothing, she still always kept her dignity and respect. She made something out of nothing and provided for her four children and other people's children as well. There would be times when we had just two days to move out of an apartment or either be set out on the sidewalk by the sheriff, but at the last minute, mama always made miracles happen. I do not know how she did it, but she never let us down. We would not have a penny in the house, but she would always hug us and say, "Don't worry because everything will be all right, and I will never let my kids go without a roof over their head." We used to be scared when we heard a knock on the door thinking it was the sheriff coming to put us out. Within hours of the deadlines, my mother pulled up in a U-Haul moving truck telling us to start moving.

We didn't ask her how she made these miracles, we just started moving our furniture into the new house. I remember those days so vividly and there were quite a few times such as these. Whatever friend that lived with us, also learned to depend on my mother to make miracles. We actually did get set out of our apartment on about two occasions. When this happens, the sheriffs come into the house and set your furniture and all your belongings on the sidewalk, and it did not matter if it was raining, sleeting, or snowing outside. We would suggest that we go to the shelter, but my mother would say, "As long as I am alive, no kids of mine would ever step foot inside of a shelter." She would tell us to go over to one of our friends' house for a few hours and that she would come back and get us later on that night. Times were so rough that if she could not find any money or place for us to stay, she would just get us and our friends to move our furniture right back into the apartment the sheriff put us out of. A day or two later, she would find us a new apartment. After those times happened, she vowed to never let that happen again, and she stayed true to that promise. She was a true survivor and the strength that was in that little lady really amazes me. She was made of mountains and had the courage of ten giants. I wonder what she was going through back then taking care of four kids by herself with nothing but a welfare check. I wonder how she made it. Me and my siblings used to complain a lot, being ungrateful not understanding how hard it was for my mother. Whenever something went wrong, we always looked to her for the solution, and most of the time she did not let us down. When things seemed hopeless, and we did not know where our next meal would come from, she would be in the living room pacing the floor, smoking a cigarette, deep in thought rubbing her hands together. She would put on her coat and leave, then come back with food and things we needed.

Sometimes she would get exhausted and go to sleep and start on her journey the next day. We would go to sleep worried, but she told us not to worry because everything would be okay. We got tired of seeing her worry, so we would gather and make suggestions such as, "mama you can go and ask aunt tee so and so for money." But she would only say, "I have been taking care of you all without help all these years and I will keep on." That was true, but we still had to worry because it was only 20 days before the next welfare check and less than ten days before we got evicted from the house.

Regardless of all these hard times that we were faced with, my mother still took care of other people's kids who were poorer than we were. Memories from these days surface from near and far. Tone hated my mother's kind heartedness when he was with her. Nevertheless, my mother stood firm on her resolutions and told him to either put up with them or leave. Sometimes he would even leave for a few days. Our adopted siblings would feel guilty and apologize to our mother because they felt guilty about it, but my mother would console them and tell them, "Don't worry about that, you are just like one of my own kids and if a man can't accept my kids, then he has no business being with me in the first place." Therefore, my mother made many sacrifices for them just as she made sacrifices for us. They lived under her care for many years usually until they were grown and could move into their own apartment somewhere. My mother was their parental guardian until then. She did what was required for them as a mother. She would tell them, "I know I can never replace your biological mother, but as long as you are living with me, I will be all the mother that you need." I guess this is why they respected my mother the way that they did. I used to wonder why she was always taking care of someone else's kids. My mother just had a kind heart. She always made sure that they knew they were loved and cared for my her. Full of mercy and kindness, she was a mother to many people's children.

~ MAMA CAN ACT A FOOL TOO ~

Chapter 7

My mother was the nicest
woman in the neighborhood, but

when she drank beer, she could become one of the wildest women in sight. She could take on new characteristics when she was intoxicated. Sometimes, I used to be embarrassed when she used to drink. Drinking did not affect her in a way that she would lose all common sense because everywhere she went, she took at least one of us kids with her to look after her and remind her. We would go over to someone's house and they would all be up drinking, and all the sudden an argument would break out. The grownups would all start acting crazy, and my mother was always in the thick of it. My mother would be acting so wild that no one could calm her down. People would tell us, "You better take your mother home." They knew that we could not do nothing, and then she would get upset with them and say, "Don't be trying to tell my kids what to do. You need to worry about your own kids." Then she would start acting wild with them. I would pull on her arm and say, "Come on mama, let's go home." Her reply would be, "Boy don't rush me. I will go home when I get ready.

You got that!" We would be up for hours trying to get her to calm down, but she would not budge. When we did finally convince her to go home, she would have her coat on and we would be leaving, then someone would make a smart remark and she would start up again. Then we were stuck for some more hours while they acted up. My mother only weighed about 120 pounds, but she would challenge these people's whole family to a fight. A lot of people were used to her when she got drunk, but new people that we met did not, and they would think she was crazy or something because she acted so wild. We would be in these people's homes in their neighborhood, and my mama would get into a family brawl with them, then we all had to fight them. It was crazy and did not stop until the police came or neutral bystanders would finally break it up. It amazes me that no one ever got seriously injured during these family brawls. They say that God takes care of babies and fools, and He took care of my mama every time she would get drunk and do unsafe and outrageous things. To someone who is not familiar with life in the inner-city ghetto, this may appear as a strange thing, but where we grew up in the poor urban neighborhood, this was common.

When people did call the police, my mother would be at the table calmly drinking her beer. I used to get worried because I knew she would act a fool with them too when they got in her face. She would start cursing them out and they would take her to jail for disturbing the peace. They always made her do twenty hours and let her go the next day after she sobered up. My brother and sister made sure that everyone went to school, and when we got home, she would be there cleaning up acting like her regular self. She often did not remember the details of how wild she acted the night before. But even when she was drinking, if one of her kids needed her or was in danger, she would get her act together real quick and come to our assistance. Her motherly instinct would instantly take over. Of course, we disliked when she would drink beer, and sometimes we would pour it out, but someone else would come over with some beer sometimes. Her and the other grownups would be up playing cards and listening to music late into the night. At home, we knew what to expect when she got drunk, but when in public, she would be unpredictable. It did not embarrass us at home because we were her only audience then. She would narrate stories of her life to us then. I took great interest in her childhood and teenage years because I always wanted to know about my mother's life. We knew my mother's habits when she was drinking. If she went to the store or a lounge around the corner here and there, we would have to go in the lounge and get her because she would be in there arguing and fighting sometimes, and someone would come get us and tell us to come get her. When she would see us, she would calm down. Only so often did we have to fight for her when someone had started something with her. We knew if she was the aggressor, and we would just take her home then. We were her sober counterpart, and our presence reminded her who she really was; our mother. That is why she probably kept one of us with her when she was drinking. We would look out for her. It did not matter what condition she was in because no matter how drunk she was, we loved her, and she would always be mama to us. When she was sober, she would be humble and sweet, but when she got intoxicated, mama could act a fool too.

~ TILL DEATH DO US PART ~

Chapter 8

Six long years my mother was with Tone. Us kids had been in great despair figuring that we were stuck with his shadow of darkness reigning as king of our household, when lo and behold, the sun shined and cast his dark shadow ashore. A good king, who was fascinated with my mother's beauty and eloquent style, decided to overthrow the tyrant king that was oppressing us. The new king wanted to conquer our throne and rule in all fairness. Normally, when a king decides to conquer another king's castle and seize the throne, there would be a war. When this tyrant Tone was overthrown, there was no battle because he was not a righteous ruler, and the queen and her offspring voted unanimously to entrust their throne to the new king and enthrone him as a king of the castle.

As for the queen, she was temporarily caught in between the possible battle and conquest, and two men who both wanted to claim her. She knew whom she wanted, but her guilt and mixed feelings of love prevented her from dethroning her old mate in an undignified manner. Such behavior did not beseech a queen to give possession of her throne to any king who has not fought for it and rightfully earned it. The prospect of love overpowers rationale and quickens emotion towards the pursuit of passion and adventure. The queen had already embarked on many adventures with Tone and his charm was now bankrupt. However, his challenger had a lifetime of charm to offer her. So how does she loyally choose between the two? They knew that this was no ordinary queen because she was very special and unique. She had them more smitten than any other queen they had met in the past. So, who was to be crowned king of this queen?

Destiny and fate has the last say in this matter. Circumstances were at work that caused Tone to lose power. A simple fight was his downfall. This was the beginning of the end of his rule on the throne. Furthermore, his ruin was shining through the light of another source. The last fight that

Tone had with my mother was when he put his hands on her; she and her offspring united forces to beat him down in defeat, and he was removed from the throne. This was our last and final onslaught against this tyrant. He destroyed his kingdom with his own hands. During the interval of his final departure, another king visited the castle and determined that he wanted to establish himself in this kingdom. His first visit was to see us kids, and after he saw the bond between our mother and kids, he decided that he could take up residence with us. So, when the former tyrant king tried to come back and recapture his throne, he was met by a fierce king who was determined to remain on the throne. He challenged Tone to battle and to fight for the castle, but Tone was so belittled and defeated that he put up little resistance as he looked into the eyes of the queen in unbelief. The new king quickly launched an offensive and smashed the old king. In humiliation, he retreated and never came back to try and reclaim his former kingdom.

After a celebration that he was gone, the queen's subjects were joyful and welcomed the new king with open arms. He accepted the queen's terms and was inaugurated into his office as king. This was the first man that her kids felt was worthy of their mother. He handled all of the responsibilities that were required of him. For the time, we actually knew that our mother was happy with a man. She kept a smile on her face, and he had her glowing. We never thought of running this man away. Our mother was finally happy, and she deserved to be after all the years of heartache she had been through. At last, a real king came along to rescue this troubled queen. The feelings were mutual, and the king was happy as well. But this was not a fairytale relationship. Every aspect of this relationship tells of the tragedies and tribulations that relationships go through in an inner-city ghetto. Despite all that my mother and this man knew, they would be together till death do them part.

A few months into their relationship, they got married. The

first six months of their marriage involved all the joy and bliss of newlyweds. This man not only cared for my mother, but he also loved her children. He was like the father that we never had around. He never fussed at us or put his hands on us. Patience was his secret of dealing with us. He rightfully claimed his spot in our family. The kingdom that he established was not without sin. Like I said before, it was founded in the bowels of an urban ghetto. This was a poor kingdom with no form of employment, no steady income, no servants, and no maids. In the ghetto there is not a lot of ways to make money, and the negative ways outweigh the positive ways. It is up to each individual to decide which way they choose to make money. Robert Brown is the husband of my mother, and he had a good heart, but he chose a negative way of hustling in life on the streets. He sold heroin long before he met my mother. This relationship was not going to change that at the time, even though she hoped that he would change his lifestyle. He was about ten years older than my mother, but he was still in his prime at this time. The problem was that he had been hooded on heroin for about 17 years. He sold heroin to support his habit and to make money. His mother stayed directly across the street from where we were living at this time.

Our entire neighborhood was infested with drugs and crime. Therefore, he was no stranger to this lifestyle. As her kids, we did not like that he was involved in this lifestyle, but still we respected him for the man that he was. After him and my mother got married, he moved in with us. It was not a big wedding; it was just a formal one. At this time, my mother was not worried about anything because she had found her soulmate. We were happy because she was happy. We were still poor, but Bobby Brown took good care of our family. After their marriage, it was time for us kids to start school again. It has always been a tradition for kids to wear new clothes at the beginning of each school year. We were always too poor to afford new clothes, until my mother married Bobby Brown. He paid for all of us new clothes. Now we could keep up with the latest trends and fashions of our peers. We admired Bobby Brown, despite his involvement in drug dealing. Our mother was head over heels in love. Each morning she would come into the kitchen smiling, shining, and acting gracefully. She really slowed down on her drinking because her husband did not like how she acted when she was drinking. Whenever he was in a really good mood, he would drink with her, and he was the only person that could calm her down if she started acting wild.

Family members on both sides objected to their relationship and especially their marriage. His family had reservations about her because she already had four children. My mother's family objected to him because he was a drug dealer with a heroin habit. My mother and him withstood those protests and did what made them happy. Both sides of the family protested for years, until they finally realized these two were indeed made for each other and it was destiny. After our family really got to know Bobby Brown, they took a liking to him and realized that he was the right man for Dee-Dee. Although they continued to object to his involvement in drugs, they still welcomed him in as family.

Bobby Brown never hit my mother. If he got upset with her, he would just leave until the next day. He was always patient with her and vice versa. Whenever they did argue and mother was in the wrong, he would swallow his pride and love his little wife all the more. Their marriage included all the ups and downs, changes and turn arounds of every marriage, and it had its defects. But they encouraged each other to remain strong during these trying times because they were as one till death do them part.

~I BROUGHT YOU INTO THIS WORLD AND I WILL TAKE YOU OUT~

Chapter 9

As my mother enjoyed the first two years of her marriage, her kids were growing up fast. Her eldest two children were not much of a problem, but it was her two youngest sons that she was concerned about. At this point in life, she was very much in control of her family. This period also marked the beginning of the many tribulations that this family would have to undergo. My mother was a very small woman and all her kids had outgrown her while they were still in junior high school. She has always been a very beautiful woman and everywhere we went people would think that she was our sister. People who did not know us at all would think that she was just one of our friends. While out in public, she always had to carry her identification because no one believed that she was actually in her mid-thirties.

The older that us kids got, the worse our behavior came. Me and Shawn were her problem children. Me and Shawn look just alike in facial and physical characteristics. As a single mother, she did her best to raise us right and tried to teach us to do something good with our lives. She tried her best, but we thought that the streets had better things to offer us than our home did. Our mother proved to us over and over again that she loved us more than anything or anyone in this world. As for our part, we were just like many other rebellious children of our generation and did not realize the mountains of unconditional love that our mother had for us.

Back when I was in school, the principal could whip the students who were acting bad in school. They also had a juvenile officer named Smitty who used to whip us with a wooden paddle when we acted bad in school. Shawn and I stayed in trouble, so we always got whippings from the principal and office Smitty. At other times, my mother would come up and whip us in front of the whole classroom. After all of these disciplinary measures failed to straighten us up, she began to wonder what it would take for us to get our behavior right. As I look back on these days, I see the cause of a lot of the troubles that go on in the world today. There we were, ungrateful children blessed with a mother that loved us more than she loved herself, and all we did was stay in trouble and take her through a lot of stress and pain.

During our adolescent years, she kept trying to raise us right. She took measures that were necessary to discipline us, but she usually was passive with us. It was only when she got drunk that she would aggressively voice her opinion, but when she was sober, she was calm and humble in making her complaints known, even when the circumstances should have caused her to be outraged. Basically, she would just hold everything inside until she drank and then she would let us know how disappointed she was with us.

When she would tell us to do a chore or something, and we would mumble little remarks and be lazy, she would just be patient with us. We were hardheaded and all of her sisters and friends would tell her, "Dee-Dee, you better quit letting them kids run over you." As time went on, she began to drink more to show us who was boss because in her normal state, it was only her nature to be patient and understanding with her children. Over the years, our behavior got worse and the family had more problems, so she began to drink more often than she used to.

I was about 12 years old at this time. I still had a keen ear for her, and I always sat down and listened to her narrate stories of the past and her dreams and visions for her family. Ever since I started behaving badly, she used to tell me, "Boy you better listen to me because you only got one mama and there is no one who will love you like I do." She was trying to stress the importance of me needed to listen to what she was trying to teach me. Somehow, she began to sense that her kids were growing outside of her grasp of control, and she began to make such statements as, "I brought you into this world, and I will take you out."

Though I was only 12 years old, I really thought that I was grown already. She sensed this attitude coming from her kids and she did all that she could to keep us in our place. Our behavior began to get disrespectful towards her and authority figures.

My older brother and sister were pretty much decent children. She was very close to her daughter. Her oldest son was 16 and had a baby on the way. They were examples of what my mother originally raised her children to be like. On the other hand, Shawn and I were becoming the exact opposite of what she taught us to be. This really disappointed her.

The harder she tried to steer us on the right path, we took the wrong path. Still she remained patient and caring for her kids. She had no favorites and she loved us equally and the same no matter how bad or good the other was. Whenever we needed her, rather she was sober or drinking, she was there for her children.

Now I know why she used to tell us, "I brought you into this world and I will take you out." There was a symbolical meaning behind this, she would never cause us any harm. The deeper meaning and understanding that I interpret this statement to mean is that she brought us into this world good, and she would take that bad part out of us. That is what she meant when she used to say to her children, "I brought you into this world and I will take you out."

I BROUGHT YOU INTO THIS WORLD AND I

WILL TAKE YOU OUT

I brought you into this world and I
will take you out

This is what my mama told me the
day that I raised my voice at her in a
shout
She said that if I ever raised my voice
at her again
Was the day that my funeral plans
would begin
The contents of this poem is based on
a true story
For the magnificence of it my mother
gets all the glory
My mama would always be the one to
smack me in front of my friends
I couldn't retaliate, so this was a
battle that I could never win
Sometimes my mother would make
me so mad
Then she turned right around and
made me glad

I remember I used to make smart
remarks under my breath
She would get her belt out and whip
me under a shelf

When I acted bad at school, mama
would spank me in front of the class
I learned my lesson at last
I was a hardheaded child
Every time I disobeyed my mother,
my punishments became less mild

My mama was always the one to put
me in check
Besides God, she is the one person
that I have to respect

She knows just how to deal with me
when I get out of line
When she gets through, I will be sure
to mind

Mama knows my habits better than
anyone
She knows the things that I do to have
fun
She also emphasized to me what
mama drama is all about
When she said, "I brought you into
this world and I will take you out"

~**HUSBAND IN CUSTODY**~

Chapter 10

With the marriage of my mother, our family saw some good times, but along with the good times came the bad ones as well. Our family was used to hard times, so we adapted. The effect from the causes of all these bad times began to take a dramatic effect upon my mother. She always kept a smile on her face, and it seemed as if she was pleased with her circumstances, but she was not happy on the inside because her world was crashing in on her.

We were advancing in our teenage years, and although we cared a lot about her, we didn't listen because we were preoccupied with our lives as all teenagers are. Her marriage was beginning to see some sour days. Burdened with bad children and a husband that did not understand the pain they were causing her took a heavy toll on my mother. She did her best to raise us right and she taught us to behave good, but the older we got we did the exact opposite of what she taught us. In addition to our misbehavior, she was also experiencing problems in her marriage now. Things took a turn for the sores because her husband did not understand the grief that he was taking her through. My mother and sister were best friends as well as mother and daughter, and they talked about certain things, and she would tell her small details about her marital problems. I learned later in life that these problems started when my mother began to feel that her husband was giving more attention to his drug habit than their marriage. His drug habit was becoming so bad that it was eating holes in his legs because he was shooting heroin into whatever broken vein he could find. He had been addicted 17 years before he met her, but she believed that she could change him and get him to leave the drugs alone. Women often think that they can easily change a man's lifestyle, but if the man is not ready to change, he will not. If a man turns to drugs, his wife is bound to think that she's not pleasing him enough. She stuck by his side and continued to hope that their future would get better. Carrying this hope in her heart, she was determined to stand by her husband no matter what trials may have lied ahead of them. Wondering why her husband would turn to drugs and not just be satisfied with her love and affection, she began to search for answers. She should have known that quitting drugs was not going to be easy for him. His habit only seemed to get worse.

My mother was doing all that she could to keep everything together, while we were all doing what was bad for us, tearing things apart. More and more, she felt helpless and her efforts were failing. Of course, this all had damaging emotional effects on her, so she turned to beer as a source of comfort. Remaining in a constant state of anxiety about losing her husband to an overdose and her kids to the streets was causing her world to get darker and darker. She was no longer able to hold her discontentment inside and signs of worry and stress started to overtake her. She never kept a secret from her kids, so she began to disclose these things to my sister. The rest of us were blind to what she was actually going through, and we only caused more problems.

Many of her husband's friends were overdosing and his habit was the same as theirs, so she did not know what to expect. There was a lot of danger on the streets. She worried whether he would get shot, killed, or locked up. Her husband sold his drugs away from home, but he still was taking a chance with his life. The only advantage that he had was that he was older, and the authorities were mostly focused on the young drug dealers who were flashy and attracted a lot of attention to themselves. We moved from the street where we were living at first and moved into a two-story apartment. For the first time in our lives, each of us kids had our own rooms. We were upstairs and our mother's room was downstairs. We had better living standards as well. Despite his faults, Bobby Brown did provide for us. But living fast always catches up to us sooner or later. The law caught on to Bobby Brown and started watching him. They were keeping tabs on all of his movements as well as his associates. Calculating his every move, the police were mounting up enough evidence to build a solid case against him. He was a relatively small drug dealer caught up in the monopoly, but when the police finally arrested him, they made it seem like he was some kind of drug lord when they put the story in the newspapers. They obtained a search warrant for his grandmother's house and kicked it in. The same day him and my mother were pulling off, the police spotted his car and arrested him. They let my mother go and requested to search her home. She allowed them to search her home, and when they found nothing, they left her alone. In his grandmother's house, they seized a quantity of drugs, guns, and more illegal things. They also arrested his brother. My mother was very worried. When she pulled up driving the car, we knew something was wrong because her husband usually always drove the car. She was barely able to contain herself as she made a lot of phone calls trying to find out where he was and if he had a bond or not. She found out that he did not have bond, and since he had already been to prison, he would have to go back again. This really hurt my mother and she did not even try to hide the pain. Knowing how alone she would be without her husband; she did not know what to expect next. Her world felt like it was closing in on her. It would be hard on her in the future without the man she loved. She never prepared herself for this. She was aware of the consequences of his lifestyle, but she was not actually ready to deal with the consequences. She was a strong woman, so it was only her sheer will that got her through this tragedy. She visited her husband on visiting days and spoke to him on the phone. She was there for

him in every way that she could be.

Now with her husband in custody, she

weathered the storm and braced

herself for the tribulations that were

ahead.

~Mama Doing Time

With Her Husband~

Chapter 11

As far as my memory serves, I recall my mother doing jigsaw puzzles and sewing. She spent a lot of time in her room doing these things. Occupying herself with these hobbies helped her to deal with her husband's absence from home. In a sense, this lifestyle kept her confined to her own personal prison. Dealing with her pain and problems in solitude offered some means of comfort. The outside presented more ugliness and problems for her, so she stayed in her room a lot doing puzzles and watching television. Jigsaw puzzles offered her a way to use her mind to concentrate on something else rather than worrying about things that were out of her control. Her kids never really realized all of the pain that she was in. She began to do so many puzzles that she had to hang them all over the walls of the house as a form of artwork. My mother was the kind of person that was grateful for every favor that was bestowed upon her. She used to say, "I may not have much, but I make the best out of what God has gave me."

Kids have a strange way of expressing their care and concern about their mother. To check on her, I would go in her room and call myself helping with one of the 1,000-piece puzzles, but in actuality, I would be messing things up and getting on her nerves. She used to tell us, "I know my kids like a book." That is true. Communication between mother and child is always beyond words. When we would check up on her, she sensed what we was doing. But out of us four kids, I am the one who got on her nerves the most. She would be sewing or something and I would go into her room and start rearranging her patterns and telling her she should do it this way or that way, but actually I was messing things up and she would run me out of her room. I would always go in her room and interrupt her, then she would stop what she was doing and just give me that stern look that mothers give. I knew what that look meant, so I would find something else to get into. Although my mother disliked me getting on her nerves, but whenever I was not at home to get on her nerves, she said that she missed me being there getting on her nerves because the house was not the same without me there.

When I got in trouble at school and got suspended and I would be the only kid at home, I was on her last nerve until school got out and I could play with my siblings and friends. It put a bad reflection on her that me and my little brother kept getting put out of school. Not understanding that it was not her fault she searched for answers to our behavior. We were not neglected at home and we were provided with love, shelter, food, and care. She taught us to be good at school and chastised us when we didn't, so she was out of solutions to the problems of our behavior. She would ask us why we were acting up, but we always made a bogus excuse and gave evasive answers because deep down inside we knew we were wrong. The talks she gave us were felt at the time, but when we went back to school and got in the spotlight, we went back to being the class-clowns. Although we were not intentionally causing her pain, the result of our actions did just that.

Her husband had to spend three more years in prison. She went through some serious changes while he was absent from home. She kept a lot of this stuff on the inside. On the outside she found a lot of things to smile about, but as long as her husband was in custody, a piece of the puzzle to her domestic life as missing. While he was in prison doing time, she was also at home doing time while waiting on him.

~DEALING WITH HER CHILDREN'S PROTEST OF HER HUSBAND~

Chapter 12

Days turned into months and months turned into years as my mother began to slowly adjust to the temporary absence of her husband. This definitely was not an easy adjustment and it was a very difficult and painful period for her. Nevertheless, she bore these years patiently and remained her dynamic self. Her children knew that she was going through some things, but they knew there was nothing that they could do about it. Everyone in her household longed for the day that her husband would be released. So, she waited patiently for her husband to come home and we all waited with her.

She maintained her same daily schedule and routine. She would get up at 7:00 every morning and fix a cup of coffee and cook us breakfast. Not much of an eater herself, nevertheless she always cooked a lot of food because each one of her kids had big appetites. She would sit there at the kitchen table with my sister and plan their day. If all of us were in on her plans, us boys would object to her plans saying, "mama we was going to do such and such today and what you are talking about doing is boring." We would pout under our breath, but once she made her intentions known it was final. She would read the newspaper and collect grocery store coupons planning months ahead. All of this was for our benefit, but we saw it as old fashioned. After she ate maybe a half sandwich for breakfast, she would clean up the entire house. Her and my sister were like a team because she would always help her with the cleaning. The majority of the time that they cleaned up, us boys would end up messing up the house before the day was over. Reflecting on this also makes me think of how kids do not understand. We just mess things up not thinking much of it. Parents, mothers in particular, make many sacrifices for their children who do not take time to really appreciate things the way that they should. My mother went through a lot of pain on my account since the day I was born, and when I think about my childhood, I regret having been such a worrisome child because I could have lightened her burden.

Within six months into her husband's incarceration, my mother decided to move again. This was the second time that we had ever moved into a house. Before we moved, we took her through a lot of stress. But sacrificing her own happiness for her kids' sake was nothing new to her. While her husband was at home, we really had nothing to complain about except minor things that all kids do. When he went to prison, my mother had to support and take care of him. The only means of support that she had was from the proceeds that she received for us. We were now getting three monthly checks in her household, and this was the most money that our family ever saw. The days of struggling off of a welfare check that the rent took 80%, were behind us now. My mother used to send her husband hundreds of dollars in prison and we were jealous and uptight about this. We had selfishly forgot that her husband had supported our family in every aspect when he was free. My mother always tried to do the best that she could. As kids and as adolescents, we would only worry about playing and having fun, while she would be sitting around racking her brain trying to figure out how to pay all the bills and maintain the household. We did not understand the facts of life, but she remained patient with us. The phone bill gave us more ammunition for our complaints. Whenever he called, we had to get off the phone so that they could talk. His phone calls made my mother really happy, and she always looked forward to his phone calls. When he did call, she would light up like a Christmas tree and smile from ear to ear. We never stated any complaints to him directly; we go to our mother with the complaints. We knew that our mother loved this man and vice versa. After they talked, she would be happy all day and for several days afterward. He cheered her up and kept her going as well as brightening her world up. Their relationship always seemed old fashioned to us. Of course, they wrote many letters to each other and she went to the prison to see him. Not knowing about love, we did not understand their relationship back then.

As me and Shawn's behavior worsened, she started taking us with her when she went to see him at the prison. He used to warn us about the consequences of our actions and point out the fact to us that prison was no place for a human being. He told us that we did not want to end up where he was. Our mother hoped that by seeing what it looked like inside of a jail, we would steer right. Teaching us by example, she wanted us to somehow see where the life we were attempting to live, would lead us. I assume that she talked to her husband about our complaints concerning the phone bills and all that stuff, but he never directly approached us to discipline us about these things. He would just direct his complaints to our mother. So, she was caught in the middle of a domestic war between her husband and children. She always played the role of peacemaker and made compromises for both sides. I must admit that us kids were the aggressors in this domestic war and the negotiations were always worked out in our favor. Being a man of principle, her husband accepted these unfair terms for the sake of his wife's children. We caused strain in the marriage also, and he never liked when we were stressing our mother out. Still he never raised his voice or acted unjust towards us. The only rare occasions he would make his authority known, was when we were being too unfair and putting too much stress on my mother, and he would then take a stand for her and not for himself. He also made many sacrifices for us over the years. Honestly though, we missed him a lot too when he was in prison. We could not wait until he got out. The protest that we launched were futile and stemmed from selfish childish motives that stemmed from us kids thinking that our mother's love should only be shared amongst us. I guess we forgot that she needed love too.

~WHEN A MOTHER WITNESSES HER CHILDREN TAKE THE WRONG DIRECTION~

Chapter 13

My mother was now 33 years old and was losing control of her kids as each day went on. I was now 12 years old and Shawn was 11. I had been in a gang for two years already. We were warned against this, but we were just doing what almost every kid in our neighborhood was doing. My mother knew a little about our gang culture; she saw us wearing the color that represented our gang and in the language that we used. When our friends would come over, she would tell them, "Don't come in my house with that gang stuff." We had now moved into a different house again. In our neighborhood there was always trouble. She loved her house and she went on about her regular schedule. Always the first one besides me to wake up in the house, she would hear me creeping around and come out of her room and say, "Bobby what are you doing? It is too quiet so you must be up to something sneaky." So, she would go into the kitchen and fix her some coffee, cook us some breakfast, and read a newspaper. Just then, everybody else would be getting ready for school. My oldest brother had already graduated and moved into his own apartment with Nichole, who now had their daughter. Nichole was originally my sister's friend when she first moved in with us, but then her and Mike got involved. Since we first met her, she was like a family member and my mother raised her as if she was her own daughter. We had another adopted brother named Alquinn, who had lived with us for several years also. My mother raised him as her own son as well. They both lived with us until they were grown and able to move out on their own. Trouble brewed and our house was shot up again by rival gangs. My mother was worried because we had a newborn baby in the house. Nichole gave birth to my mother's first grandchild, Miesha Bostic. My mother was only 32 years old and she was a grandmother already. My mother liked Nichole, but she did not like her ways. I remember when Nichole was pregnant, my mother would keep up with what she was doing and eating and telling her and my brother Mike to quit playing so rough around the house. Knowing that she was to be a grandmother gave my mother ultimate joy, and it would open a new chapter in her life. It also filled some of the void her husband had left. She would wake up in the morning making plans for her grandchild as if she was the one giving birth to the child. Nichole did not mind because she was a child herself and knew nothing of raising a baby for real. So, after several months of planning, Nichole finally had her baby, Miesha. My mother was overwhelmed with joy when she was born. Miesha was the center of attention in our household. Everybody had great hopes for her. As for the rest of us, at this time my sister Marquise was in her last year of high school, and I was in the seventh grade, and Shawn in the sixth.

Whenever we used to bring our friends over and the music would be loud, my mother would come in to see what we were doing. We would always say that she was being nosey or in our business. She would tell us that our business is her business and we better watch our mouth before she smack the taste out it. By this time, we had started bringing our friends over without any discretion, and the more lenient that she got, the bolder we got. Another problem that came up was that we moved a lot and my mother would move on a block that was the opposite gang that we were in. So, these gang members would shoot up our house and tell us that we had to move. But we never did. So, one day about twenty or so gang members kicked in our house with guns drawn looking for me and my friends, and they shot up the house. The irony of this situation was that me and my friends were only 12 years old and these other gang members were grown men in their late teens and early 20's. But age did not make any difference to them. They were Crips and we were Bloods, so they told us to quit wearing red in their Crip neighborhood. Hardheaded, I continued to wear red endangering everybody. The new house we moved in was in the hood, so this only led me to get into more trouble and getting worse in our street activities. It was very disappointing for her to see her kids take the wrong direction in life right before her eyes.

She had foreseen that we were heading for trouble and this scared her. Every night she would begin to pace the floor and look out of the window until we came home. Only when we walked in the door, would she lay down and go to sleep. We told her to stop tripping because we were cool. We did not understand why she was stressing so much because we were only handing in the neighborhood everyday just kicking it. Nevertheless, her motherly instinct made her worry about her kids. She would watch the news and see that some teenager had gotten shot and killed near where we would hang out at, and she just wanted to make sure that we were okay. My big brother and sister started telling me and

Shawn that we needed to quit worrying mama so much. By this time, we were too far into the streets and was not paying attention to these reprimands. My mother made sure that we stayed in school because she figured this would keep us off of the streets and out of trouble. But what she did not know was that for us, school was just another place to engage in gang activities and show off.

On a personal level, she was counting down the years until her husband would come home. Me,

Shawn, and Al just considered that we were hanging out having fun and it was no big deal. Nevertheless, the anxiety that we were causing our mother began to show on her face. I regretfully admit that we had a rebellious attitude during our childhood and convinced ourselves that our mother was trying to run our lives. We did not consider the fact that our mother clothed us, supported us, fed us, sheltered us, loved us, and cared for us. But in rebelliousness, I guess we thought we could make it on our own out there. This is the problem with teenagers and adolescents today. So instead of listening to her warnings, we got worse. But everything that she warned us about became a reality. We would just blow it off as bad luck or something and keep hanging on the streets. I know that it caused her much grief that the very same babies she bore in pain and carried for nine long months and sacrificed for all these years, were now disobeying her righteous orders. Here we were at 12 years old, throwing our lives away to the streets. My mother had by now stopped physically whipping us, and even when she did that, I do not think she liked to whip us. Back when she did whip us, if we cried too hard, she would cry with us and apologize and tell us that she did not like whipping us, but we were being too bad. Now she was without a remedy to really steer us right. We were two hardheaded sons who would not listen and could not imagine what we were taking her through. No words can explain a mother's pain when she knew her kids were endangering their lives and freedom every day, while all she could do is pray for them, worrying about their safety. It hurts when she feels powerless over their destiny and can't control them. So, these years she had to endure the emotional and mental trauma of seeing her children take the wrong direction in life.

~THE DISAPPOINTMENT OF A MOTHER WHEN KIDS TURN TO THE STREETS~

Chapter 14

My little brother and I were mother's heaviest burdens. As we ran the streets, she stayed home worrying about our safety and future. Her main concern was that we be guided alright. Our only concern was hanging out and making money so we could keep up with the latest trends and fashions of our day. She took good care of us, but we wanted more so we could emulate the neighborhood drug dealers. Although we were provided with love, care, and attention at home, we still were blind and thought that no one in the household really understood us. So, while our mother was at home worrying about us, we would be across town acting a food as if we did not have a care in the world. She always warned about the consequences of our actions and soon we would find out what she was telling us. My older siblings were not perfect, but they obeyed her rules and respected the house. Long ago, my mother tried to show us that jail awaited youngsters like us and that this is not a place that we wanted to be. She had an idea of what we were out there doing because she knew what the guys, we were hanging out with was about, plus my sister's friends were local neighborhood girls, so they would be telling my mother the things we were doing. Soon, I would experience her warnings about the criminal justice system. I was caught with a gun a few months after my 12th birthday, and I stayed in juvenile detention for a month. Then I was sent to a group home called

Hogan Street under the Division of Youth Services for troubled youth. This really hurt my mother. It was already enough that her husband was locked up and now her son too. Shawn did not learn from my experience because he was out selling drugs. Thus, her burden was getting even heavier.

She visited me every week and always wrote me and let me know that she was there for me and I was not alone. She was very disappointed and hurt that I was at that place. During my stay there, my eyes were opened a little. For the first time, I saw what she was going through. It was only when I was taken away from the streets that I begin to look at the bigger picture. I told myself that when I got out, I would get her to quit smoking cigarettes and drinking. I planned with all my heart on doing this. When I came home my mother was so happy. The love and care on her face spelled out to me that she deserved a lot more than her kids were giving her. With this small portion of understanding, I told myself that I was going to try and make things better at home. Now that her family was reunited, she could rejoice and forget some of her other troubles.

Men had always taken notice and interest of her. Now they were flirting with her more than ever. When I got home, Shawn and Al were selling drugs. I stayed clear from all trouble for a few months, so she was happy to see that I was doing good. I was even making A's and B's at school. I was using my intelligence for the right reasons and behaving the way that she had raised me to be.

Soon though, I was becoming other something other than what she raised me to be because I gave in to the temptations of the fast money in the drug trade. It did not take her long to find out because I started buying jewelry and fancy clothes while putting gold teeth in my mouth. Mostly everyone in the neighborhood knew who the drug users were and when these people started knocking on her door looking for her kids, my mother knew beyond a doubt that we were selling drugs. I was the first that she confronted because she was so disappointed that I had been doing so good at home and school. I had let her down. I was still doing good at home, but my involvement in the drug game was overshadowing the good things I was doing. When she confronted me about my drug dealing, I felt really guilty and tried to evade her. She had witnessed that good child underneath that she had raised and then to be let down by my present drug dealing was too much for her. I knew I was wrong, but the money that I was making caused me to ignore my conscience. As the weeks passed, she continued to deal with the disappointment of my actions. When I used to walk in the house, she would give me that look that always messed with my conscience, so a lot of times I just stayed away from home and spent more time in the neighborhood. She would always tell me that as soon as the police caught up with me, I would be going back to jail. But I thought that I had it all figured out and they would not catch me. She would say, "Bobby you need to slow down out there in them streets because when the system gets hold of you, there ain't nothing I can do about it." It hurt her that we had chosen this lifestyle and were selling drugs. She used to ask us why, but we had no legitimate answers. I remember the hurtful looks she had when the drug users would knock on her door looking for us to buy drugs. We told them not to come to our house, but they would come anyway. I would try to say that they were coming over for other purposes, but she would ask me what is a grown man twice my age knocking on her door looking for me for? There were no more excuses to give. It was obvious what we were doing. Therefore, she experienced a lot of anxiety about us. She would wait up for us to come home every day and if one of us came home without the other, she would ask me where Shawn was, and I would tell her that he was on Beacon at such in such house. She would ask me why he did not come home with me and I would tell her she was tripping because he was cool, but she would worry until he came home. Back then I never understood why she was worrying so much.

It was very difficult for her to be losing control of us and it seemed that there was nothing she could do about it. Every solution that she came up with seemed to fail because we were more interested in hanging on the streets. If going to juvenile detention for six months could not change me, then what could, is what she wondered? Shawn, Al, or I getting killed out there was her greatest fear. But in our young immature minds, we always assumed that nothing would happen to us and she was worrying too much as always.

~SHE IS ONLY HUMAN AND SHE MAKES MISTAKES TOO~

Chapter 15

Pressure, stress, anxiety, loneliness, and pain were just some of the emotions that began to take their toll upon my mother. The world felt like it was closing in on her. She needed a way out. She wanted a better way of living. How could she find this better life? Her problems at home were mounting. Everything seemed to be out of her hand, including her two sons. All she could do is hold on and pray that things would get better. In the meantime, she tried to figure out what she was doing wrong. Was there any strategy that she had not tried yet? Or was she just trying wrong things to better her domestic situation? Why couldn't her kids listen to her? Why couldn't they see that she wanted what was best for them? Why had they turned to the streets, and what did the streets have to offer them that they were not getting at home?

There were the questions that ran through my mother's mind as she searched for answers. Having a war within herself when she was not the cause of it was stealing her peace. Every day she would marshal new forces to the front-line, but they would be defeated at the hands of her rebellious kids. Every time she would launch her frontal attack of unconditional love, care, and concern for her kids, her offensive would be met with the defense of rebellion, stubbornness, and hard headedness. This was unhealthy for any mother. This was painful because she loved her kids more than she loved herself.

She was our liberator, but in our rebellion, we treated her as the oppressor. She was engaged in a war to save our lives and we were so blind that we would run counter to her loving force while destroying her and ourselves at the same time.

She would give her own life just to protect ours. So why did we prefer the danger of the streets rather than the safety and love at home?

Why couldn't she get her children to see the light? Why did they want to live in darkness? The walls of the small world that she lived in with her family were rapidly closing in on her and she had nowhere to run to except to the love that was in her. She did not know how to hurt; all my mother knew how to do was love. Searching for some way of release, she ended up finding comfort in a man. Being deprived of her husband for three years was very difficult for her. At 34 years old, she was still beautiful. In pursuit of relief from her intolerable domestic situation, she concluded that she needed to have some fun and deserved to be able to go in the world and have some fun too. After all, she was only human. What about her kids though? The answer to that question prevented her from living to the fullest for many years. For the past 18 years, she deprived herself of a personal life because her kids were her life. Now her mind began to compromise. It concluded that her kids thought they were grown anyway, or at least were behaving as if they were. They were buying cars, jewelry, and living away from home for extended periods of time. Still these were her kids and they needed her, whether they knew it or not. Still she reasoned that she deserved to get out in the world and have some fun also. Before she could do this, she had to deal with her conscience because she was married, although her husband was in prison. Would she forsake her marriage just because she was tired of waiting and wanting to have some fun? Eventually, the pursuit of adventure and companionship won the moral battle and she decided to have an affair.

Her niece introduced her to a guy named Stan, and for all intents and purposes, he seemed to be a nice guy. He was outgoing and humorous and seemed to be just what she needed to escape the pressures of home. So, she started dating Stan. He took her out on a lot of fun dates. He showed her a lot of the fun and good times she had been missing over the years. Every day when he got off work, he would come over our house and get her. At first, she gave him a trial period. She had to show him that she was a mother and had priorities to raise her kids. She had to show him her domestic situation and her place in it before she would get deeply involved with him. Furthermore, she told him about her husband, and he had to know that whatever they shared could only be a temporary thing. So, once she knew that he understood all that, they started a relationship. Us kids did not mind, we just wanted to see her get out of the house and have some fun. We stayed out of her business and hoped that she was having a good time. We remained a part of her conscience as well and whatever we thought was important to her as well. In the end, she reasoned that she deserved to have some fun if even only for a few months. Besides, she figured that she was not going to get emotionally involved with this dude. It would only be temporary. What my mother did not realize at that time was that her little affair with Stan would lead her down a destructive road. Stan had started using crack cocaine. At first, he was able to conceal his habit, and then she started to develop some real feelings for this dude. He told her that he would quit using this drug. On the contrary, his habit only got worse. He would come and get her after he got off work and bring her back later on that night. And that was their pattern at the beginning. She acted like she was happy, so we were relieved that she was finally having a good time, and not sitting around stressing all day. After a while, things between Stan and my mother began to look strange to us kids. We had no proof that anything was going on, but we stayed on high alert to make sure that he caused our mother no harm because we found out that he was smoking crack. If he had caused our mother any harm, we would harm him really bad. She assured us that everything was fine. I reflect on how me and my brothers were quick to physically hurt anyone who even said so much as an unkind word to our mother, while at the same time we were causing her the greatest pain internally. We were protective of her, yet we did not protect her against our own actions of rebellion. This is something that I had not recognized until recently now that I am mature enough to see things clearly. In a desperate attempt to regain control of her own life, she sought to get out in the world, and she did this by involving herself with the wrong man. Her relationship with Stan took a turn for the worse. Somehow, she got involved in using crack cocaine. We sensed that something was not right with her an we started watching her movements. We then did all that was in our power to keep her away from this dude Stan because we assumed that he got her to use crack cocaine. Every time we found out that she was with him, we tried to find her and bring her home. Now it was our turn to worry about her and we felt a sense of apprehension when she left. Shawn, Al, and me were selling crack cocaine and it was hard to live with the fact that our mother was using it. It seemed like it was only then that we really started to pay attention to her like we should. At the beginning her habit was light. On the other hand, Stan had already got out there really bad. Whenever my mother was high, we automatically knew because of how different she acted. This was something that we really hated. We figured that if we could get her away from Stan, that she would quit using, so we boycotted him from her, but they still found ways to spend time together. Blocking his phone calls from the house did no good either. When she did leave home, my sister would be calling all over town trying to find her and we would be driving all around looking for her. we knew that she could take care of herself, but that did not console us. We were used to our mother being at home. When she did come home, she would be feeling guilty, so we knew that her and Stan's relationship was not based around good things. She loved us and the guilt was really getting to her, and she did not want us to see her using drugs, so she moved into my brother's apartment and he moved back home with us. Stan's sister lived not too far from his house, so she was still with him all of the time. I remember we would question as to where she had been and she would say, "Boy don't question me. I am the mama and I am the boss around here, now where have you been?" We went over there to check on her on a regular basis. My sister called her on the phone several times a day.

Within a few months, we found out through Stan's sisters that he was putting his hands on my mama and we would search for him high and low, then beat him up really bad. But she still had feelings for this dude and would go back to him. We still beat him up when we saw him. We were not going for any man hitting on our mother. Them days were over with.

By this time, we had to move again because the landlord was fed up with me and Shawn's illegal activities. My mother was still messing with Stan for a few more months, and she was still using crack cocaine. Stan had got arrested for a string of felonies and was sent to prison. My mother came around to her senses and went back to her normal self. This was a dark period in her life. She made mistakes and learned from them. During that dark period, she had lost herself while trying to find herself. This was a different period for us because we had never seen our mother on drugs until then. So of course, we were relieved when she got herself together. No matter what she did, we always loved her, and she will always be our mother. We understood that she is only human and made mistakes too.

~WHEN YOU'RE YOUNG TEENAGE KIDS THINK THEY ARE GROWN~

Chapter 16

Adventure with her corrupt male acquaintance caused a great setback on the domestic scene. When she moved back home, me and Shawn were now way out of control. We actually thought that we were grown, or at least that is how we were acting. Although we still lived under her roof, we did not abide by all her rules. I know she was upset with us, but at this time, she was also frustrated with herself because of her personal faults and dealings with Stan. She figured that, had she been at home those few months, that me and Shawn would not have gotten as wild as we had been. Back at square one, she started admonishing us about our actions and telling us to slow down. Again, she warned us about the consequences of our actions. We never talked back or got smart with my mother because she would not go for it. We respected her, but our behavior was disrespectful because we were selling drugs and always had our friends over. She would always tell us, "Those people that you are running the streets with do not care about you, and when something goes wrong, mama will be there." We knew that these words were true, but we were so hardheaded. She continued to be patient with us. We were her babies in her eyes no matter how big we got. In our youthful rebellion, we found futile reasons to keep living the way that we were living, and the streets were everything to us. If we were not hanging on the block, we felt like we were missing something. That was where all the fun was at, and where we thought we had to be. The grief and disappointment of my mother was overwhelming, and it was the same way with our friend's mother's also. For us, making money was everything. She never supported what we were doing, but when we used to come home with lots of money, she would tell us to do something meaningful, but we did not listen then either.

This is the folly of the kids of this generation. We think that our elders are trying to run our lives and be in our so-called business, but their maternal instincts are to protect us. Our mothers have our best interest at heart. We are so misguided in our rebellion against our mothers. We say such things as, "mom is old fashioned and does not know what she is talking about," or "she needs to find her some business," etc. Here we are children between the ages of 10 and 17 and think we know everything. I apologize to every mother that has to go through this with your children. I apologize for each one of us. Please forgive us. In the end, us children cannot escape the wrath of the consequences for being rebellious against our parents.

I do not know how my mother had the extraordinary strength to keep on loving and cherishing her children with every inch of her soul, while we were being bad and rebellious. It is hard to understand how that little lady did it all by herself, but she kept on loving us unconditionally, regardless of the pain that we caused her. What was it that made me and Shawn think that we were grown? This is a question that she so often asked herself and tried to find the answers to. Somehow, we foolishly thought that we could make it in this world without any help, but our mother knew better than that. She knew that we would be lost without her. She loved us too much to let us find out on our own the hard way. So indeed, she mustered all of the grief and pain that we took her through. We tried to tell her that she did not have to worry about us because we were fine on the streets every day, but I know that you cannot tell a mother to not worry about her children, especially children like us who were hanging on the streets all of the time. In our ignorance, we somehow figured that we were independent of her love, care, and protection. All of this despite the fact that we still were in junior high school and lived under her roof, eating her food, and resting our heads in a bed that she paid for. The only thing that I paid for in that house was my clothes, jewelry, and my car parked outside. The furniture that we found comfort on, heat that was keeping us warm, she paid the bill, the telephone that we stayed on day and night, she paid the bill, but yet we ignorantly considered ourselves as self-sufficient and behaved as if we were grown. We did not even have respect for ourselves in our stupidity.

At 14 years old, I moved out of my mother's house and moved in with an older friend who was twice my age. He was a somewhat legend in the neighborhood as a gangster drug dealer. This was my role model. This caused my mother lots of anxiety not knowing where her child was at, and she had heard some negative things about this guy I was living with. I was going to clubs and driving around in luxury cars, and doing all kinds of crazy things, and some of it was getting back to her. She figured that it would only be a matter of time before I met my demise.

My mother never had time to worry about her own well-being because she was too worried about us. She began to stress a lot and was smoking a pack of cigarettes a day. I stayed away from home about a year, until I got arrested again. All the while, Shawn was in the streets doing some of the same things I was doing. We were lost in an illusion that would bring about our ruin. Our mother knew that we loved her, but we did not take the time to understand the pain we were causing her. She would never give up on us regardless. All she could do was wonder what happened to the kids she had gave birth to and raised the right way. Questioning herself, she wondered what had taken place inside of her kids minds that made them think that they were somehow grown?

~REUNITED WITH HER HUSBAND~

Chapter 17

My mother tried to improve her domestic conditions because her husband was soon to be released from prison and she wanted to offer him something better when he came home. Through and between the tremendous stress that her kids were causing her, she had a spark of hope of better times with the presence of her husband soon to be in her life. Just the fact of knowing that he was coming home kept her happy. He promised her that when he got home, things would change for the better and she wouldn't have to worry about all the problems that she was having now because he would straighten things ups.

She continued to try to make things right at home before he got there. Every day she was getting things ready at home for him because she wanted to give him a warm welcome. He had been in prison four years. I was now 14 and my mother was 35. I had, by this time, moved back home. After having been on the streets on my own for a year my behavior was really out of control. Shawn was also causing havoc. We both loved her and always recognized her status as our mother, but we had a strange way of showing her our love. Our priorities were all backwards and the only person in the world who seemed to care about our well-being is her. Doing all that was in her power to correct us while we were too ignorant to realize that we were taking the wrong turn was hard for her. The only relief that she had present was knowing that her husband was on his way home. This is how she maintained her strength during this period. Surviving the stress and pain with the inner happiness of knowing that she would be reunited with her husband kept her strong. Despite all that we were putting on her, she was still so happy. I remember when he got out, she acted as a child who had received his first bike. He was first released from prison to a halfway house. Her husband was finally home. She had waited a long time for this. Now that this time had come, she was overwhelmed with joy. We silently watched her shine with all that inner joy that made our mother shine like the sun. More than anything, all of her children knew that any happiness she got, she deserved it.

Her and her husband made a lot of plans and began to complete them one at a time. Their present holdback was that he was still confined to this facility. He used to come home a few hours a day when he got off work before he had to report back to this facility at night. My mother used to watch the clock every day and say, "I can't wait until 3 o'clock when Bobby come home and you all better get rid of your friends because you know that Bobby do not like a house full of people when he comes home." We complied with those requests because we all wanted him to have a warm welcome into his house. Prison was hard and we all were glad that he was finally home. She would cook his dinner and have it ready for him every day when he got home, and we used to tease her about it because she would put everyone out of her room and clean up the house and make sure that everything was right for when her husband would walk in. Smiling from ear to ear at 3 o'clock she would be so happy. We would smile with her because she was happy.

We were all teenagers now, but the thought that our mother was in love was funny to us. Her and her husband seemed so old fashioned to us and we always reminded her of this. She would just wave us off and say, "My kids better go and sit down somewhere. You all do not know what you are talking about." It was a relief to her to be free from the stress that we were causing her, and she had a chance to focus on her own happiness for a chance. Finally, at least for a while she could focus on her marriage.

True to his word when Bobby Brown got out, he had established himself as a good role model and he and Shawn and I began to show respect at home. Keeping all of our wrongdoing on the streets, we only came home to eat, sleep, and change clothes. Things surely changed for the better when he got home. He was working every day and not using or dealing drugs. This was a great relief to our mother that he was being a good model for us.

In fact, my mother did not allow much to make her upset or destroy her joy during this year. She did not drink much, and she kept her same schedule. I remember she kept that little smile on her face. Being determined not to let anything destroy her well-deserved happiness, she just wallowed in her own bliss. There were not any secrets she kept from her kids, so she implemented many new policies and reforms in her household and told us the purpose of them.

Making her wishes known and proclaiming her position, she would tell us, "It is no secret." I recall her saying that statement to us as far back as my memory serves. There is a lot of slogans that she coined precisely for her and her children that we all understood very well.

Being a deep thought thinker kept her quiet and in meditation a lot. Concerned about getting bills paid and her children's well-being always kept her mind occupied. Although she was doing all of this for our sake, in our state of ignorance we paid these things little attention. My niece Miesha was about four years old now. Miesha was a grandmother's greatest joy and she was the only one in the household that did everything that my mother told her to do. Nicole, her mother, had moved away and left her so my sister and mother took care of her. My mother was walking around on a cloud of happiness and within these months, changes in our household were in order.

Bobby Brown respectfully maintained his position as head of the household. So far, he had made good on all of the promised that he made while in prison. He and his wife were having such a good time every day. They were going out to the movies, plays, etc. They were acting like teenagers going on their first dates. I remember she used to come home telling us what they did. Her happiness was evident as she recalled the day they had spent. It was kind of funny to us because the things that she was telling us they did seemed so old fashioned and boring to us. When we made a mockery, she would just smile and wave her hand and say, "My kids are just jealous" or "you all do not know what you are talking about, me and my husband be having a good time."

I must admit that she did look stylish stepping out of the house when he came to pick her up, and she could always out dress us and look young at the same time. She still looked like she was her kid's sister.

When her husband walked, we would really bust out laughing because she would be bragging on how good he looked. At first, he would be looking around wondering what everyone was laughing at. As he finally found out that we were laughing at them, he would take his little wife by the arm and they would walk up the streets all smiles and not pay us any attention. The harder we laughed, the more our mother knew that we were jealous. But her and her husband would be enjoying themselves like love struck teenagers. Our mother was just happy to be reunited with her husband.

~THE PAIN OF A MOTHER WHEN HER CHILDREN DISRESPECTS HER~

Chapter 18

My mother always kept up with the times and she always remained young with her kids. She was a part of us in every way. Wearing all the hairstyles and clothing of our generation, she looked twenty years old, but we still called her old fashioned. Never did she forget her duties as a mother. On the contrary, it was her hardheaded children who forgot that they were still her children. Her whole personality permeated with unconditional love, care, and mercy demanded that we give her the utmost respect. Instead, as each day that passed, we became more and more disrespectful.

By this time, we were smoking weed and drinking. Everywhere that we moved, we became a little bolder with our actions. We knew that our mother knew that we were getting high, so sooner or later, we bought our weed smoking into the household.

My mother barely used to come out of her room, and she would be in there sewing, doing a puzzle, or watching television. The only time that she would come out of her room was when we were making too much noise. She would run us out of the house, but when she eventually found out how crazy we were acting out on the streets, she would rather us be in the house blasting the music getting high because at least she knew where we were at.

I remember she would admonish us every day and remind us

that we could not go over to our friends' house and clown in their mother's house. Knowing that she was right, we would still make some lame excuse.

Seeing us doing these things around the house, she would just admonish and give us a hurtful disappointed look. We were too high to pay attention. Our behavior and disrespect became so outrageous that we began to have no discretion. We began to keep drugs, guns, and weed in the house. Her knowing what we were doing on the streets made her on the edge every day. Her husband had been out almost a year now and the things that her kids were doing were so unfair that she could not ignore our actions anymore. The happiness that she was receiving since her husband had come home was slowly deteriorating. That joy was being stolen away because she had to worry about her kids.

Shawn and I just started exceeding all boundaries and we lost respect for our household. We were selling drugs on the streets and eventually the people that we were selling to, they found their way to our house, and when we told them not to come there anymore, they still did anyway. Our greed led us to sell to them.

The things that we were doing were really taking a toll on my mother. We were really hurting her. Having tried everything in her power to get us to straighten up, it all began to weigh her down. It was hard to enjoy herself in her own house now because her sons were always doing something that they did not have any business doing. So now she had to sit in the front room and look out of the window and see what we were doing. Every day something was new, our behavior only worsened while we were causing our mother more pain and grief.

How could the kids that she gave birth to disrespect her the way they were doing? This question crossed her mind as she looked at us and saw what we had become. In turn, this made her look at herself and wonder what she had done wrong in raising us. For her, she could not come to terms that it was not her fault how her kids were living.

Telling herself that there must have been something that she was doing wrong, she searched for answers to her son's actions. It hurt her too much to ask us this question in her normal mind set, so she had to chemically alter her mind state by drinking beer in order to ask us.

No matter how corrupt and grown I was acting, she always knew that I was her child who would sit down and listen to her whether she was drinking or sober. She knew how to work on my conscience, but she was wondering was it doing any good now days because I was still carrying on my negative actions at home and on the streets. There is no one in this world that can get to my conscience or make me upset the way my mother did, and I wonder if she knew that?

So, she would sit me down and tell me how she felt. Looking at me in my eyes, she would ask me why? "Why is you and Shawn out there selling drugs and carrying on?" Now how could I answer this question coming from my mother? The one person in this world whom I owed the

greatest respect to. I had to give her

an answer though. I felt her hurt, so I

had to say something; after all, she is

my mother. What could I say though?

I could not evade her question and her

questioning eyes were burning

through my conscience. I was telling

myself that I had to get away from

that house. I can't see my mama like

this, so I reasoned that I would leave

for the night and come back

tomorrow. Still I couldn't avoid her

question and I had to give her some

kind of answer that was truthful in my

eyes.

I would point out to her that all

the other kids in the neighborhood

had more than me and my siblings

and it was our turn to have something

in life, and selling drugs was the only

way we could get it. I told her that I

was tired of us being poor and seeing

her trying to take care of us off a

welfare check. I told her that I wanted

to have my own car, girlfriend,

jewelry, etc.

She would just kindly remind

me of all the sacrifices that she had

made for us throughout our lives and that we did not need to be out there selling drugs. Reminding me that she could and would provide for us was not convincing enough for me at that time to stop my actions. I would not give a reply of rebuttal when she told me that she would sit up at night worrying about us and our safety while out there on the streets. My guilt was becoming stronger and I knew that she was telling the truth. For the moment I could feel her pain and knew that what we were doing was wrong.

This never stopped me from engaging in the activities that I was involved in. I would keep away from the house for a few days and then I would soon be back at it. When I tried my best to be respectful in her household, she was happy with the fact that I was at least trying. Despite these times I was still continuing on in my wrongdoing. My course of action saddened her. I really let her down. It hurt her after talking to her kids whom she loved more than herself, and they continued to carry out this negativity. What was she to do?

Again, she resorted to the only relief that she could find, and she began to drink again more regularly. It was too much to see her kids running over her. As I said before, our mother was a very humble lady. In her sober state, her dignity prevented her from acting out and releasing some of the anger and pain that was stored up inside her. So, in order for her to somewhat release all of what was stored up in her, she had to alter her normal mind set in order to lash out at us about our actions and her

disappointment at what we were
doing.

Only recently was I blessed
with the insight to understand why my
mother smoked so many cigarettes
and drank beer. All month she had to
put up with us, day in and day out.
Courageously she withstood these
tribulations that her children took her
through. I now wonder how she did
it? Made of mountains, she had the
strength to go through it all. Most
mothers let their children go when
they think that they are grown and get
too far out of control, but our mother

was too attached to her kids and she could not let go.

Day after day, we would strike a blow at her loving and forgiving heart. If we were not in the house doing something unauthorized, then we were on the streets and she worried until we came home. If she had to choose, she would rather us be at home where she could keep an eye on us. During these years, most of our friend's mothers had already given up on them and put them out. My mother's love was too strong for her children to let them be in the world on their own. Hers was such that it was beyond what we can even think of to this day. Her love was too strong and pure for this corrupt world. No words can grasp or even begin to explain the unconditional love that is in her. The sweetness and kindness that was in her, rubbed off on anyone she encountered. Through her adulthood, she had taken care of other people's children and gave all that she could to anyone she saw was in need. So, nothing would make her let go of her children no matter how wrong they were in the things they were doing.

~I CAN ALWAYS DEPEND ON MAMA~

Chapter 19

Since I was a child, I always knew that no matter what happened, rather I was right or wrong, I could always depend on mama. She would always be there when I needed her. Regardless of all the stress that we caused her, it never prevented her from coming to our aid and being right there for us. I remember she used to tell us, "Whenever everybody else turns you down, mama will be there." Constantly she reminded us that she was our only true friend. There were days when she used to see us getting in the car with someone who she knew was in trouble and she would get in front of the car and prevent us from going anywhere. I would tell her that I was just going around the corner, but her motherly instinct felt that something wrong was going to happen. All mothers have this instinct and they are normally right when they have this feeling. A lot of children are rebellious and try to ignore this maternal instinct as just being too protective or trying to run our lives. Little do we understand how much our mothers love us. Each time that she told me something would go wrong, and I went against her intuition, the very thing that she warned me about would take place.

Instead of heeding to her warnings, I would just tell her that she was worrying too much. She would just sit there and give me that look that only a mother gives you. I love my mother dearly, but I did not always show it in my actions or like all kids, I had a funny way of showing it. Her concerned looks always burned through my conscience even when I was in rebellion. The most obvious thing that allowed me to escape my conscience was the marijuana and liquor that I consumed on a daily basis. I would get lost in my high or go out on the block to try to forget what she was saying. When she sensed danger, she would watch me real close and sometimes even try to keep me in the house. When I did get in the car and leave, she would give me a look that made me feel really guilty. Shawn would be feeling the same way as he sat next to me in the car. She would shake her head at us and all we could do was look ahead and light up some marijuana to salve our conscience.

Whenever things would go wrong like she warned against, she never said, "I told you so." She never threw it up in our face. Not caring what she was up against, she would be there for her children even if her own life was in danger. When the police would call her and tell that we got arrested, she would drop whatever she was doing to come and see us and see if she could get us out. She would say to us, "Boy I do not understand why you all just keep getting into trouble." We had no real responses because we knew we were tripping out there. But as soon as we got out, our homies would come and get us. The neighbors liked my mother and they respected her. However, they did not like the way that we were not respecting the neighborhood by selling drugs and stuff. They were getting fed up with us and would voice their concerns to my mother. She would tell us and warn us to stop. A lot of the other guys our age was doing the same thing, so we all continued to do what we were doing. We were not discreet, and we played really loud music from cars and loitered on the sidewalks. The elders got fed up with us youngsters and they started calling the police on us every day. We would just run and get rid of the drugs and guns when they came. Therefore, they started watching us real close. The police knew that mother did not approve of our actions, but since they could not catch us on the streets, they decided to surveillance our house to get a search warrant there. The neighbors' complaints of us would not go unanswered. The police eventually obtained a warrant and conducted an early morning raid. They tore her house into shreds looking for evidence. They even ripped through the walls. This outraged our mother, but all she could do was watch as the police ram shacked her house and destroyed her most valued possessions. When they left, the entire house was in disarray. They found just a very small quantity of drugs and guns in me and Shawn's room. We were not there, so the police had a warrant out for our arrest. When we got home, she was stressed out and was very worried about what would happen to us. All we could say was that we were sorry. She was also very upset because after the police found the drugs, the city of St. Louis confiscated her house and told us that we had to move in ten days. Calmly she just cleaned the house up and salvaged what she could that the police had not totally destroyed in their search of the house. Me and Shawn got arrested the next day. She came to see us and then went home and looked for a new place for us to live. Once again, she had to move, and something that she valued was being taken away from her because of her kids' careless actions. She was never resentful towards us, although she was upset. This was the last house that we got her put out of. While we were in jail, she was there for us and trying to get us out. She just wanted us to do right. Even though we had disappointed her, she still was there for us. She showed us that when things went wrong, we could always depend on mama.

~THE PROBLEMS OF A TROUBLED FAMILY~

Chapter 20

One of my mother's most sacred hopes, only her most close kept dreams is her four children would stick together. There was nothing that she would do to see some family unity. I have always known her to dislike when we quarrel amongst each other. In her eyes, her little family is her nation. A nation that she started, and she felt was her duty to keep this nation together. This small nation consisted of her four children and three grandchildren. My sister gave birth to two children. My mother named both of them and she even gave them special nicknames that we will always call them by. She was so attached to her children that she would not let go, even once they were grown. As her own children advanced into adulthood, she then turned her energy into raising her grandchildren. In them she saw a second chance of raising her kids, but this time better than she did the first time. These children provided her with great joy. Unlike her own kids, they obeyed her rules and listened to her. When she looked at them, she saw a younger version of her kids.

In our youth, we as her kids, did not uphold the standards of family unity the way that she wanted us to. Everybody was kind of doing their own thing. By this time, me and Shawn were released from juvenile. My mother had not found us a new place to live, so all seven of us had to move into my brother's one room apartment. This put a big dent in my mother's pride, but throughout her whole life, she had endured struggle after struggle. There was nothing else to do but be the strong woman that she had always been and taught us to be. She never broke down in front of us or lost her composure no matter how emotionally torn she was inside. When we were all crowed in this one-bedroom apartment, she remained her normal self, going about her daily schedule as usual. Even in the small quarters of this apartment, she used a negative situation as a positive, in that she found the ultimate joy in being surrounded by all of her four kids and grandkids. We were the most important thing in the world to her and as long as she had us, she was okay. I regret having gotten her house taken because me and Shawn were selling drugs there. Our mother forgave us. I know that it hurt her that we wasted so much time in the streets. Somehow, she knew her kids' potential and she always recognized our gifts even when we were too lazy to develop them. Ever since I was a very young boy, she told me to use my mind to become someone. She had this intuition about her kids from the start. She was very much in touch with us and recognized the gifts and skills that each of us possessed, and with the dismal resources available to her, she tried to cultivate our talents. I never knew why she used to try to push me hard to use my intelligence in school. This is why it really upset her that I was spending so much time in the streets wasting my life away.

Shawn and I were born nine months apart, and for two months of every year, we were the same age. Every year at this time we would increase our fights among each other. It was a senseless sibling rivalry thing where we would argue since we were the same age. During these two months, then I was not the "big brother" at that time since we were the same age. As kids, we fought about any and everything like a lot of siblings do. My mother really hated this. She never liked the tradition of siblings fighting and arguing. This used to really bother her because all she ever wanted was some family unity amongst her children. Her favorite words to use were, "Ya'll make sure that ya'll stick together no matter what."

On the streets, Shawn and I went back to the same old neighborhood across town and got back involved with the same stuff. In spite of this, she never gave up on us. For the most part, we kept our street stuff away from home. My mother and sister rallied against me and Shawn and would daily reprimand us for our street activities. In our rebellion, this caused a split in the unity of the family. We were still as one, but it was like different factions as me and Shawn were in our own little world while my mother and sister were attempting to steer us right counteracting our wrong activities. We just ignorantly saw this as an attempt of them being nosy. As the streets grew colder, so did me and Shawn.

Meanwhile, the disunity in our family was reigning high at this time. Our mother continued to try and implement better policies to ensure the safety of our home. We saw things in another light and felt that our family was targeting us without just cause. My mother's marriage was also experiencing its ups and downs; more downs than ups. Her husband Bobby Brown had drifted back into his old habits and started using heroin again.

His habit was getting worse daily. Unknowingly, she turned to herself for answers and wondered what she was doing wrong in her marriage that led her husband to turn back to drugs. I do not know why she blamed herself. Bobby Brown would come home lost in his own world and act very withdrawn. She felt shut out of the world that he was in. She loved very hard, so it was difficult for her to understand why he was diving back into the abyss of heroin addiction. Sometimes when she asked him what was wrong, he would tell her that her kids were the problem. Since they met, he had patiently allowed her to always put her kids before their marriage. Seventy-five percent of their arguments involved her kids. Ninety percent of their arguments centered around her children. He was rightfully tired of seeing her go through what she was going through on account of her kids. Through the years, he had sympathized with her desire to do all she could to keep her kids on the right path, but as they got older and worse in their behavior, he figured she should allow them to get on the streets and learn on their own. He wanted him and his wife to get their own apartment somewhere else while paying the rent for her kids to live with each other. Here was the woman that he loved more than anything and vowed to spend the rest of his life with, unable to detach herself from her kids. This worked on him in two ways. It caused him to love her more and admire her more for the unconditional love that she has for her children. On the other hand, it bothered him that his wife would always put her kids before him and their marriage no matter what. Since he married her, he always knew this and accepted it. This is understandable while her kids were young. But as they got older and started acting grown and causing her all this stress, he felt that something had to change. He was tired of seeing his wife worried about her kids. He worried about us also, but in hindsight there was no quality time left for them. He was tired of this. What little time they did have left was strained because every time they were together and along, she was confiding in him how she was worried about her kids. Any married man expects to be able to enjoy at least a few hours with his wife and enjoy her company in a time where they just exclusively comfort one another. Ultimately, this left her torn between making a choice between her grown kids or her loving husband who supported, loved, and cared for her. Not being able to tell him in words that may hurt him or seem harsh, she would just evade arguments with him about her kids. She knew that it hurt him flat out that she would always put her kids first.

The pain of his would show on his face, and he would leave until the next day. He just accepted that she would always put her kids before him. In turn, he would be right by her side as she was there showing her support for us.

Her husband loved her with all of this heart and soul. For many years, he laid next to her and witnessed her sleepless nights, while comforting her trying to assure her that her kids were okay wherever they were on the streets, and that they could handle themselves. He would put his personal complaints to the side most of the time to comfort her. During the times that the frustration would intensify, he would threaten to leave if things did not change with her children. Sometimes she feared that he would actually leave. Still she was unable to let her kids go, even the grown ones. Her husband was the one that paid the bills, but she would risk it all for her kids. In his heart he knew that he would not leave her, she was his soulmate and life would not be the same without his wife.

She would tell us kids that we needed to consider her husband's feelings. All of these things combined were putting rifts in the family unit and causing disunity. These are the problems that we were experiencing as a troubled family.

THE PROBLEMS OF A TROUBLED

FAMILY

There's a lot of problems in a troubled
family
The greatest tool that they are missing
is unity
Only if they would stick together
They would be able to survive the
storms of any weather

Family is one of the most important
things on this earth

These are the people that have been
around you since birth
There is so much drama in a family
that is troubled
When they fight against each other,
their tragedies are doubled
I love when a troubled family stands
by each other's side
Forgiving each other's wrong and
letting go of their pride
Taking a standby each other whether
they are right or wrong
That is just an example of a troubled
family being strong

In a troubled family, things seem to
fall apart when they couldn't get any
worse

This family feels like they are under a curse
How much more heartache must they endure
They have been through enough hard times for sure

If you are on the outside looking in, their struggles may seem unbearable to you
What else can they do
They have endured pain all of their lives
They just keep telling each other, everything will be alright

A troubled family doesn't necessarily have to be a broken one

They still have each other after it is all
said and done
When I write this, I am writing about
me
I am a member of a troubled family

~IT IS NOT YOUR FAULT MAMA~

Chapter 21

As the problems in the family
increased, my mother again looked to
herself for answers. She muttered
such statements as, "Lord what did I
do wrong raising my kids and why did
they turn out this way;" "What could I
have done different while raising

them;" and "I did the best that I could with what little I had." I still cannot understand why our mother blamed herself for our actions. When I learned that she blamed herself for our faults, I told her that she should not take that burden up on herself. Her kids had their own minds, after she raised us and taught us right, it was up to us what we did later on in life. This did not assure her because she still somehow thought that it was her fault the way that her sons lived their lives.

Her kid's adult like attitudes and behavior began to take a toll on her and she again started drinking heavy. Over the years, she had always smoked cigarettes and drank beer, but during these times it got worse and now I understand why. When she drank, it allowed her to vent her frustration at us. The chemical in the alcohol enabled her to transform her normal humble state of being into a state in which she could aggressively lash out at her children and show her dissatisfaction at our actions. Through the alcohol, she was able to show us a mirror of the hurt and pain that was going on inside of her. The reflection of this mirror gave us a reflection of her pain, and in turn, it became our pain. The guilt of this was too much for us to deal with.

We hated to see her drinking, not just because of how she acted when she drank, but because when she drank beer, her actions gave us a clear view of the hurt that was stored up inside of her, and our conscience was working on us and we felt guilt, but in a way that we did not want to admit. In her state of intoxication, she would tell us the truth about ourselves. The reflection in this mirror was one that we did not like to look at. It did not matter who was around; she spoke her mind. When drinking, she did not allow us to act all crazy, and she demanded her respect. If we acted like we did not hear one of her orders or requests, she would get physical with us with whatever was at her disposal, and there was nothing we could do but accept what she was dishing out verbally and physically.

When our friends were over while she was drinking, she would really make her authority known because usually they would be disrespecting her house when they were behaving as if they were grown. While she was chemically unbalanced, she would tell them off with no exceptions. Inside they knew that she was a loving respectful lady, but she would put up with them hanging out in her house all through the month as if her house was their home. She was also fed up with these disrespectful kids, and she stood up for all the other folks of her generation that were tired of these disrespectful children who acted like they were grown and showed no respect for their elders. So, she would lash out at them physically and verbally for their outright disrespect of her house. She would say to them, "Did my kids tell you who run this house? Get your damn feet off my furniture. You better show some manners in my house." We all were just typical delinquent teenagers hanging at home getting high, but during these times, she was not going for it.

While she was sober, all of this was kept inside. There were times that we thought we would get into it with our associates because some of these people were wild and she would smack one of them for saying a curse word around her, and them stepping up on their shoes since she was so short, and then she would get right in their face and say, "Boy don't look at me like that, I ain't scared of you." These wild street dudes and sometimes girls would just say,

"Okay Mrs. Brown, I am getting ready to go" and they would just say, "Man your mama be straight tripping." In her they saw a reflection of their own mother and the respect that we owed them.

The suicidal way that me and Shawn were living on the streets was scary to her. People were telling her that her son already had one foot in the grave. We did not really care about death because it was a chance that we took living wild out there every day. I had just turned 16 years old and Shawn was 15 years old. He was now snorting heroin and was hooked on it. This drug swept our generation up and he started using this addictive substance. Our whole state of being worried her because we spent all of our time on the streets, which was a dangerous jungle in our city. We could have been killed every day because it was happening to our peers. Homeboys were getting killed regularly.

Worry, anxiety, and apprehension became her regular companions. Whenever we came home, she was relieved just seeing that we were still okay. During the first few months after my sixteenth birthday, I spent a lot of time at home. Of course, I was broke at this time and that is why I sat down for a while. Even though I was no longer a small child, my mother still knew my ways, I still would go in her room and ask her a lot of questions and get on her nerves. Shawn had been getting into trouble a lot also. He was purchasing cars every other month and the police kept impounding his cars because he was only 15 years old with no driver's license. My mother was fearful of our driving anyhow and thought we would end up in some serious accident. Whenever one of us had to take her shopping or something, a 30 minute trip would take an hour because she would be telling us, "Boy slow this car down," "Watch that car," "Turn that music down," "Boy that light is yellow." Every one of her kids' driving was reckless to her, and the only person she felt safe driving with was her husband. Shawn would be speeding up and down the streets, and she would look out the window and see him and say, "Lord have mercy and watch over that boy." She only rested when our cars were parked outside. Whenever we drove off, she would be worried not knowing what we were doing out there. At this time, things were so bad on the streets even we could not ignore it. I decided to get a job. Finally, I wanted to try and get myself together. I would be in the house reading the job wanted ads and my mother was so proud of me. Shawn would drive me to the interviews, and I kept searching for a job until I got one. She was really proud then that I had got a job as a photographer at Six Flags Amusement Park. I was honestly seeking a change. I was tired of the same stuff. I looked at my surroundings and knew that I had to change, so I moved to my grandmother's house in a middle-class blue-collar neighborhood. She is a very spiritual person and her house rules back then demanded I show respect. My mother and I knew that I could not smoke weed in my grandmother's house and have a house full of people and all that other stuff. There were curfews at her house too. So, my mother had some relief knowing where I was and the fact that I was trying to change. Furthermore, she knew that I was going to have to change my outer patterns at my grandmother's house. Shawn was in the streets a lot, so our house was quiet. Her husband was in and out of rehab at least trying to deal with his addiction, so things were trying to look up for the moment. This particular turn of fortune only lasted a few months. Then the calls started coming from my grandmother's house about me staying out at all times of the night and coming in high. My grandmother would not allow this, and I had changed from the young grandson she raised, and so she told me I had to move back home. My mother was happy that I was moving back home. She had missed me. When I got back home with Shawn, we started our old patterns and the peace was stilled. We were wilding out. We went to a neighborhood party and I got too drunk, and on the way home I got arrested. This was the last time I went to the juvenile detention center. The authorities certified me as an adult but decided not to prosecute the case for lack of evidence. I only stayed out three months and then in December of 1995, I was arrested for 17 serious felonies and was headed to prison for decades. I was 16 years old and my mother was devastated. It was beyond her to understand how I had gotten into this enormous amount of trouble. The seriousness of the charges really troubled her. Although I was still a juvenile, I had been certified as an adult and would face life on several counts. Logically, she could not figure out why her children made such serious mistakes. I was sad about my fate and what was to come. I was locked up with a lot of older dudes and I was one of the youngest there. She would come and visit me and say, "Boy you look like you should be in somebody's classroom, not in nobody's jail." Shawn was still in the streets being wild, but fate was soon to slow him all the way down. A few months after I got arrested, he got shot in the side and was in a coma. The doctors said that even if he awakened from the coma, he would be paralyzed from the waist down and never walk again. My mother was at the hospital everyday by his side. The thought of losing her son was causing her to fall apart inside. She looked to God and prayed for his recovery. She made a vow to God and said, "God if you let my child live, I will always be there for him." God heard her prayer and Shawn miraculously survived this life-threatening tragedy. God had spared his life and he came home. His near-death experience was not without consequences. The bullet left him permanently paralyzed.

How was she to deal with this? Was she to lose hope and grow weary now? No, she was determined to keep on living with her kids and have the best of hopes for them. Although her child was now paralyzed, she was grateful and gave thanks to God for allowing him to live. Now the question was how was she going to comfort her 16-year-old child who had been told that he would never be able to walk again? How could she make him understand that life was still worth living? Feeling his pain and knowing that there was nothing she could do about it left her heartbroken. The pain and anger was all over his face. More than anyone, she understood, and if she could trade places with him, she would. Somehow, some way, she would get him to see that there was much hope and he still had a lot to live for. Alone at night in her bed, she would look for answers. How did her two youngest sons end up in these situations? Her child was her responsibility, so she pointed the finger at herself. It could never be her fault because of the way that we were living. Yet, no one could convince her of that, thus she continued to blame herself. This was an unnecessary burden that she carried on herself. No matter how many times we told her that it was our fault, and these were the consequences of our actions, she still figured that maybe she could have done something different and prevented us from living the way that we were living. No mother should carry this guilt. If a kid chooses to disobey his mother, that is the fault of the rebellious child and not the fault of the mother. In fact, it does not even reflect on the mother. Her child chose to ignore her. So please mothers, do not blame yourself. My own mother blamed herself although we have told her hundreds of times that, "It Is Not Your Fault Mama."

I Am Not Giving Up

I lost twice and I'm starting all over
again
In the end my divine destiny will
reign
I have lost a thousand times in my life
Still I know that things will be alright

My life is not something that I can
procrastinate
I must be mentally strong so I can
motivate
My motivation is always to progress
I will not settle for less

I had to display a lot of stamina

Dealing with my own paranoia

Much of my life has been wayward

Coping with all of the things that I

had to absorb

Many moments of my life were

critical

Down to the wire it was pitiful

I have received a lot of rejections

All I was searching for was perfection

I still sometimes face sorrow

Nevertheless, I am hoping for a better

tomorrow

When life starts evaporating my luck

There's no way that I am giving up

<u>Chapter 22</u>

In her own words: Excerpts from letters that my mother wrote me:

A card that she sent me on Valentine Day reads:

For you son
"There is a special place in your heart
that only a son can own."
It seems like only yesterday
That you were very small,
But even though you have grown up,

Some things have not changed at all.

You have always been

You will always be

A son who is worthy of

The very best that life can bring

And very special love

> Happy Valentine Day
>
> With Love
>
> Mom

A letter that my mother wrote me

on February 16, 1996 reads:

Hi Bobby, I love you, thanks for the

letter. I hope that you are taking care

of yourself and staying out of trouble.

I need to know what courtroom you

will be going in before time. Mama

really was not listening to that judge; I was looking at my baby and daydreaming about a suitcase full of money to get you out. Things out here is not really well but will be okay. I do not want you to apologize for what has happened, but I hope you realize the pain you have caused me. I miss you and your well-being is worrying me. Please be careful. Why did you tell Renita (ex-girlfriend) that your last name was Johnson? I love the way you make me laugh. I can always count on a smile when it comes to you. Bobby stop writing that gang stuff. It is going to cost you before it helps. Your little brother is still in juvenile clowning. Write him and let him know that jail ain't no joke. Don't worry, I will try to have the lawyer soon, even if I have to go back to work; you are worth saving. I love you. Do not ever doubt my love for you cause my heart holds a spot that never could be taken from you. Bobby, I have always loved hard and even with men, they used me because they knew when I cared. My husband is getting outrageous with his habit. I do not think he is going to last much longer. I need you to be strong and hold on cause no one loves you more than I. Thanks for finally realizing how worried I will be about you when I do not hear from you. I will panic and start crying worrying people. Hold on, God is on the way to see mama through so she can help her child. I won't give up; don't you. There is a will, there is a way. Remember that. I have not heard from Nicole in a month now. I hope she is okay. I do not like the idea of Miesha being out of school. I am concerned about what it is doing to her not knowing where her mother is, is a

load on a five-year-old. I hope that

she go ahead and tell us something

because to keep running off leaving

this child is not right. It is worrying

me, but I do not want anyone to

know. Bobby I will not stand by and

let them throw away the key on you

because you are mine. I know you did

wrong, but there has got to be a better

way to punish you where you learn

that other people have rights too. I

realize what you did is not going to be

a piece of cake, but I know you did

not mean to hurt anyone. I keep

saying what happened going over and over in my mind, it did not happen, but we both know it did and figuring out what to do about it is something I have to accept. I will have to keep up with my grandchildren because my grandchildren will always have grandma. I will be there for them trying to make up for not being the best to you all. Please let's try to stop Shawn before it is too late. I cannot allow the pain to win this battle. You can make it and will.

Love Mom

A letter she wrote me dated

January 25, 1997

Hi Bobby, I hope you are well and living life to the fullest. I am sorry for what you did in that courtroom, but I guess you thought you were right and had to prove yourself wrong. I still love you and will always stand with you. I cannot begin to tell you how much those people hurt me, but I knew that would happen. I will not tell you nothing wrong. I want you to know that I love you and will be with you through it all. Do not give up, life has a way of working for us all. Stand tall and remember your friend is me. Be the loner that I know you are cause you staying in too much trouble to be the person I know you are for real. I will be out here trying to make it better for all of us. Ask God for the strength to go on. Bobby He will give it to you. He knows your stubbornness and hardheaded and will forgive you. He does it all the time. Hurry home, I need you. Do not worry about me, I will be alright.

A letter she wrote me dated

January 31, 1997

Hi Bobby. I am up early thinking
about you. I cannot sleep nor eat at
night thinking about what is going to
happen to a child so smart and
loveable. Please be careful. Take my
advice and be careful, think before
you make another mistake. You can
get into as much trouble in there as
out here and that worries me, but I
still love you and want what is best
for you. I ask God to hold your hand
and carry you through this for me

because my child need guidance. He

forgave you already. I am worried

about you. I love you and always will

want you here where you belong and

the day will come, just hold on and be

strong. I miss you.

Love mom

**A letter she wrote me dated March
1, 1997**

Hi Bobby. I am writing this letter out

of love to let you know that I

understand and love you no matter

what. I do not think you have meant

anything that you have done lately.

The smartest child that I had just

outsmarted himself. I am hurting for
you. Bobby I cannot agree with you
but will stand by you through it all. I
cannot lay down another night
without letting this pressure up off of
me. I keep crying and feeling down,
but I am holding on. All my life I
have did wonders with the little that I
have. I also know the pain that my
child feels. I am afraid that you are
hurting yourself, most of all me by
holding on to that stubborn streak in
you. I will always love you and
believe me when I say every day that
you are gone mama knows it and

sometimes might let it get the best of
her. I realize how much Shawn needs
me now. I will not let him down
either. I felt like yesterday was the
hardest day of my life (the day I was
sentenced to 241 years in prison for
committing robberies, assaults, and
kidnapping when I was 16 years old)
and I could not do anything about it.
Crying is hard to control, but I will try
not to because I do not want to worry
the rest of the family. I feel so empty
knowing it is only the beginning.
Bobby hold your head up and stay out
of trouble. I never knew how to hurt

anyone intentionally and nobody can

understand the things I do but I have

reasons for whatever I do. Baby If

you ever need me, you got to know I

am here because nobody loves you

better than me. I have got to find a

way to get you out of the system and

here where I know you belong. Why

didn't you listen to me? I have so

many questions, but I am in enough

pain without wondering if I am

hurting you. Because, "I told you so"

was never favorite words, not when

they came from mama. God be with

us and keep mom strong until her

young man come back home, and

remember God is walking all around

you day and night watching over you.

Bobby right now we have to stick

together and carry each other even

when this is over you got to know that

I will never leave you out there. Stop

talking and acting so crazy. Use the

knowledge that I know you have

within. If I could change places with

you, I would. That is how much I love

you. Wouldn't trade you for the

world. Be strong and don't let me

down, call me as soon as you get

there. I have so much to say and I

wonder what is really on your mind. I do not have money or power, but I am full of love and understanding. You know the old saying, "God do not put more on you than you can bear." God bless the child with its own, well that's me, I am strong and will not give up and now God has given me some strong children. Keep that thought in mind and you will make it. No matter what, I am proud of you. We will make it through this together, there is no other way. Life do not end there, it ends only if you give up, then we have a problem. This is a cruel world and the people in it is nothing what they appear to be. If I made a mistake in my life for loving my children, then so be it. I can live with that okay. I awake every morning and ask God for a better day. Sometimes I wonder if I will ever see it, but at least I asked. Hold on, keep your head up, an most of all, do not ever give up. First, I have got to accept what has happened before I can correspond with what I am dealing with. I will smile. There is a rainbow somewhere at the end. Mama will always love you. I will not tell you anything wrong. I might say something that you do not like, but I will never hurt you. Bobby you have got to know what this is doing to Shawn, he loves you so much, when one of you hurt, I hurt too. I know you are hurting because I feel it. God promised me He will give me the strength to deal with you through this. I know He will send you home with us. I know I cannot take back the life we lived, but together we can make it better. I have saw mothers lose their children and could not feel their pain because I know nothing of that, but when

Shawn got shot and God let him live,

I knew then what the feeling was of

those mothers who did not get the

chance that God has given me. So,

what I am saying is that you are alive

and He will give you back to me soon.

Hold on, out here is hell. I keep

telling you not to worry about me, I

will be alright even though times are

not getting any better. I can stand and

hold my head up and be proud of

myself though I deserve more. Do not

worry about getting a job, I can take

care of myself. I love you little boy.

You are a handful for a little person

like me to carry, but believe me, I will
be there to pick you up if you ever
feel like you are falling. Call me and
mama will try to talk you through it.
Bobby I am going to close now, will
write soon. Call when you get this
letter okay.

Loving you forever,

Mom

A letter she wrote me dated March 21, 1997

I got your letter and after we talked on
the phone, I felt better about a lot of
things. I was so happy to hear from
you baby. Bobby just stay out of

trouble. I will get in touch with the lawyers. I know how important it is to you. I have not got in touch with the public defender, but I am still trying. I will let you know something soon. Be good, help is on the way. Please stay out of trouble and away from people that might not understand you. I miss and love you more than life itself. I went to church with your grandmother Gloria yesterday and really did not understand it that well, but I learned that you cannot do it alone and that hurt because I want to do it alone. I hope we will be up there next month cause I really want to see my baby.

Well I will close for now, but my

heart is always open and ready to

accept you. It will not be long before

God allows you to be free and home

where you belong.

Loving you

Mom

**A letter she wrote me dated March
30, 1997**

Hey, I got your letter today and as

usual I glowed. Do not ever worry

about me turning my love away from

you. My love for you is unconditional

and could never leave you. You will

always be in my heart and mind. I am

trying to contact this lawyer as we

speak, and I hope that we speak by the

time I mail this letter. Did you get

your money? You will never

understand why I feel guilty, so do

not worry yourself with that. Bobby

Brown is back in the hospital.

Hopefully, this time things will be

different, and my marriage will

survive because I want it to work out

cause I am tired. Bobby please stay

out of trouble and understand what I

am saying when I say that things will

work out. God will not allow me to be

in much more pain. About that judge, forget it because my love for you is forever and nobody can change that. I keep saying that I want to run away because I am scared to die but running away is not the answer and I will live with that. I do not care about the phone bill. The only way I can be close to you right now is the phone, please call. So, call and if you ever need a friend or someone to talk to, that is what I am for, do not take that away from me. Understand that mama will always love you and be a big part of your life. I am not going anywhere.

Shawn is fine and your big sister Keeda is going to have another baby soon. Your brother Michael is okay. I will be there to see you as soon as you get where you are going. Do not worry, be strong and hold on for me. Everyday gets harder and I understand, but like you said, let's not worry. God will lift this heavy load in time to save us all because He hears when no one else does and knows what is best. So hold on. Do not forget what I said about getting into trouble, it will only make things worse. I cannot take much more. I love you now and forever. We have to

concentrate on giving this time back.

Hold that hard head that I gave you up

and God will work it out. Call me, it

is important that I hear from you

soon. I will always love you and want

you home with me. It will get better. I

wish you would get over your ex-

girlfriend Sandy and I will call her

when you call me.

Loving you Forever

Mom

A letter she wrote me dated

September 12, 1997

Hi Poo, I am sitting here thinking how much I miss you. There is nothing in this world that I love more than my children. I am still waiting for my grandkids from you and your brother Shawn. I know it seems like forever, but nothing lasts forever and one day you will be home. Just be strong and understand as long as God is walking with you and has forgave you, it will not be much longer. I realize the pain that you are in because I feel it even though I ask God every day to keep you strong and safe. I cannot help but cry because that is my job. I know my birthday tomorrow is going to be rough on me so call and check on me. I realize that visiting is one thing, but when time to go home, I take that hard when someone I love is not coming home with me. Being truthful with you it is hard because there is not anything that you can do about it. Do not worry, I do not have money to get you out of there, but God will make a way for your freedom and happiness if you just believe and have faith. He loves you too. Baby please do not ever give up. I am sorry that you got the short end of the stick, but life itself is not all that it is made up to be. All we can do is live the hand that we have been dealt and pray it will work out for the best. Every time I read your letters I cry and start drinking because I am in so much pain and I hide it behind the beer. I am so empty inside but when I look around me and see my grandkids, I know I have so much to live for and so do you. Smile Bobby, you will get out. I would rather see you there than in the grave. I am thankful for that because I see mothers that will never see their child again. So think, we are blessed already, and God can make anything possible, so hold on and do not give up on life or anything else. Shawn is trying to walk; it is going to take some time, but he will, and God has given him this. Ask and you shall receive. God is slow but He will be there to free you. I love you and nobody will ever change that. I keep every card and letter and read them over and over. I am a fighter and when I want something, I keep at it until I win. I know I taught you all the same things in life. That is why I know you can make it in there

because you have seen harder times
out here. See you tomorrow and stay
out of trouble. Come home where you
belong. God will help you. My
grandchildren are a job, but I get paid
much more than money just knowing
that I am doing the right things and
being there for them. I will not let
anyone else keep them which makes
your sister happy. I will always love
and need you in my life. Take care
and be strong. Have to get ready for
tomorrow, seeing you is all that is on
my mind right now, spending my
birthday with you, there is no other

place that I would rather be. Stay

away from trouble, hold on, be strong,

and keep the faith.

Loving you forever, Mom

A letter she wrote me dated

November 21, 1997

Hi Bobby. I was sitting here thinking

of you. I love you so much boy until it

hurt. I know that being strong is

something that you have always done.

But Bobby, be cool because in the

solitary confinement, all of the time is

not cool. Jerome is in jail and his

mother is hurting. I know the feeling

because when they took my baby, I

could have died. I will never forget

the day you were sentenced. I got new

furniture and still working on making

things better for myself. I do not have

the things I deserve, but I will one

day. I still have not found me a house

I can afford and be comfortable in

with Shawn situation. I have ten days

before they put me out this house and

my hands are full but haven't runneth

over. I have always believed that God

does not put more on you than you

can handle. I will be okay. I am not so

happy having to move again but

maybe it is for the best. I hate that you

did wrong and was so hardheaded. I know in my heart that God is going to send you home to help me with Shawn; we all love you no matter what. I do not want to speak on it now, but I have stopped drinking and feel much better. Now I pray that God will take the taste out of my mouth, but it is still there, but I have been fighting it. Bobby please stay out of trouble. Listen to me Bobby. I have a lot on my mind and God knows it is hard. I love you now and forever, well I will write some more later. Needs to find me a place to stay in a hurry. I

want you home more than anything
and one day God will send you to me
where you belong. I am so worried,
and it is so hard being strong alone. I
love you. I have not mailed this letter
yet because I wanted to write with
some good news. My marriage is
holding but the drugs seem to have
more in common with him than me.
Shawn is heavy on heroin and keeps a
room full of people, but God knows
they keep him going, but he had given
up on walking again. It hurt but I
guess he will try again when he is
ready. This is a mean world and I

must live in it. I know how much being there hurts because I feel the pain that my child is in. but I also know how strong you are. Bobby please stay out of trouble; it is not worth it. Be cool and smart, stay in those books, you are better at that than any child I have ever known at your age. I believe you will be home to live and raise a family of your own. Gotta run and put in some time house hunting. I am in pain and worried about a roof over my child's head. I worry so much it feels like time is on my hand. Bobby maybe now is the time to unlock my eyes to the things I

have always blocked out. Start putting

your birthday orders in early. I will

send your Christmas present early so

it will be there on time. Happy

Thanksgiving; eat for me. We love

and miss you. Mom

P.S. Poo when you called last night,

God lifted a load off me. It felt so

good to hear you and know you are

well. I love you so much. Thanks for

calling, please do not worry about me.

I will take care of Shawn the rest of

my life. I promised God if He let

Shawn live after he got shot that I will

always be there for him. Things will

work out for the best. Hold your head

high and pray baby God will answer

you.

Loving you forever, Mom

A letter she wrote me dated

January 13, 1998

It is another day and you are heavy on

my mind, but it will always be like

that and I can live with that. Do not

worry, you will be home soon. God is

on our side. Stay out of trouble and

hold your head up. I know you did

something wrong, but God knows that

you did not deserve what has

happened and I cannot wait until you figure out a way to give back some of that time. I love you and want you where I can see you. Mama do not believe in giving up. I believe in fighting until the end. I have never been afraid of nothing when it comes to the love of my children. I just wanted the plain life and simple things for my kids. I did not care about the good or the bad. I just cannot deal with my child doing this kind of time without reason because whatever the judge reason was it was not right and proving her wrong is all that matters to me. I will not accept

this and that is why I need you to stay

out of solitary confinement because I

know my child and the loner that you

are, but you do not deserve to be

locked up that much. I feel your pain,

it is just like that with mothers.

1/15/98 – Hi Poo. I love you and miss

you and is wondering what you are

doing. I love you and when you hurt

so do I. Pain is not a joke when it is

your heart or your child. 1/26/98 – Hi,

I am woke again. I love you, cannot

sleep, think nor eat from worrying

about your well-being. Most of all

when will it be over. My plan is to understand that no matter what, I will never give up on your freedom and you being where you belong. I am determined to have my baby back. Every time I hear Tupac Shakur record, "DEAR MAMA" I cry and think of you. I miss you.

Mom

A letter she wrote me dated January 30, 1998

Hi Poo, how are you doing. I was writing to remind you that tomorrow is Carol birthday (her deceased sister) and she is 41. Did you get the information for the lawyer yet? I miss

you and that empty space will never

be filled unless what I have is with

me. Keeda is gone to Texas and I do

not let her take the kids on her spree

because life out here ain't no joke,

and besides, I am happier when I

know where and what the people I

love are doing. Answer the questions

above as soon as possible. I refuse to

take this chance on your freedom. I

need to get started at least. Yes, I am

wondering what you are doing, how,

why, and all the other things a mother

would. I hope my husband is doing

well by me, but I can feel that

something is wrong there too, but a

person that lives inside of their heart

lives in a big place. Have you heard

from Stacy? Keeda is just being

Keeda, besides she is my only

daughter and still is trying to learn

where she is heading. Kids are

beautiful. My grandson is bad, and

my granddaughter is a leader. Well

enough about people. I love and miss

you. What are you doing right now? I

have to look for another house. One

day this will not happen. I will be so

happy with the red brick house and

white fence that no one will be able to tell me to leave or put me out. Bobby mama would not want to trade places, but for you to be here with us right now I would trade a portion of this life I am living. There are so many unreal and crooked people out here that I have to ask what the limitation of that. Hold on help is on the way. That record "Food to My Soul" is something that I expect from you. After hearing that song, "DEAR MAMA" by Tupac Shakur for the first time was when you tried to make me understand what it was saying. I

wonder what you are doing. I miss
you. My granddaughter is something
else, she wants grandma to play. Well
things are okay.

I love you

Mom

A letter she wrote me dated

February 4, 1998

Hi Poo. I received a letter from you
today and was happy to hear from you
as usual. Everything that is good to
you ain't good for you. It hurts me to
see anyone messing with mine,
especially when I cannot tell my child
what to do anymore. I do not want

you to worry about me right now. I
need you to leave those people alone
and stop being so hardheaded to the
point where you are blinding yourself.
There have been a lot of times in life I
did things I did not want to but had to
in order to make it; it is not easy. I
love you and would never tell you
something wrong or to hurt you. Do
not ever give up because I believe in
you and I need you to realize that
solitary confinement is not the answer
no matter what because it will always
be there, and you will not. I hate to
even think of you being there when

we both know how much I need you here. Hurry up and call home, I need to talk to you. One day does not pass that I do not ask God to help me help you, we all make mistakes and believe me we pay. Sometimes I feel like giving up, but I would rather give in because a quitter never wins, and I know you are stronger than that. About my drinking, yes but it is also another story because it is not an excuse. I just be feeling that is the answer to the pain in which I cannot change. Sure, I know right from wrong. I love you boy; I need you to understand that life is hard and living in this cruel world is worse. Well sweetheart, mama has to run and get these stamps now and I will write you soon.

Loving you forever, Mom

A letter my mother wrote me dated February 11, 1998

Hey Poo. I miss you. How are you? I am not fussing or anything, but it is important that you stay out of solitary confinement. I have nothing but love for you. My house burned down so I have to start over again as far as furniture is concerned, but like I always said, I might give in, give out,

but I will never give up. I have not

talked to Shawn today, but I am sure I

will before the night is over. I worry

about him because he cannot walk

and out here it is a cruel world, plus it

is cold outside. Keeda and Ms. Muff

is okay. I miss them being where I can

see them. I wonder what you are

doing and is you okay? Most of all

never will I stop loving you. I feel

nothing but pain and regret most of

the time. I understand that life goes

deeper than that in this world. When

you get this call, I really need to know

you are okay. I will send the number when I find a house. Well I am not going to be happy until I talk to Shawn so I might as well get on up and start calling around looking for him so I can feel better within. I know he is going to say I worry too much but what is a mother to do other than loving her kids the way I do mine. I will try to write everyday letting you know when I find a house. Your sister had a candle burning and the kids knocked it over, that is how our house burned down. It hurts but I am thankful that everybody made it out safe in order to stand there and watch everything go up in fire. It hurt but being strong is another story, that is what I had to do. I do not like it here, sleeping on the floor is bad business and my body is not as young as it used to be. Besides, I am just used to my own, always have been. My husband is here with me and I am glad that he did not walk out on me. I love you. Miesha wrote on this page. Call herself writing you a letter. Bobby please be good so you can help me help you. I need you out here to help with Shawn. Well I am going to

find him now. It is five after nine. I
went looking for him and did not find
him. I left him some clothes with his
girlfriend. I am worried. Will write
some more tomorrow. I have to go to
sleep so I will not be worrying about
Shawn. I love you most of all miss
you and need you here with us.

2/12/98 – I found your old letter that I
wrote you and I am mailing it. Still
have not found a house today. I talked
to Shawn today. Going to check on
him soon. Do not worry, I am still
looking for a house so I can bring
Shawn home. He needs to be with me

so I can know that he is being taken care of. I do not think that other people will see after him like I would and besides, together is where we belong. I will write more later. I love you. I paged Shawn but he still has not called back. I pray I find a house. Shawn just called back, but I am still worried about him. Things out here is not right and nobody loves him like I do. I cannot stand for nobody to mess with my kids. Well I am going to call Shawn. I talked to him and he is supposed to go stay over my sister Virginia house until I find a house.

Knowing that he is with family makes me feel better already. It is rough out here, but I promised myself that I will not give up. I love you and will write again next week. Take care of yourself and stay out of trouble.

Love you

Mom

A letter she wrote me dated February 15, 1998

Hey Poo. I was happy to see you. You lifted my spirits up and most of all I love you. Being with you bought about a change in me. I am not going to worry, and I promise I will go to the hospital and get well because I want to be here. The love that I have for mines is different from others. Knowing you will be home soon makes me strong. I just had to write you and let you know how strong you made me feel yesterday. I did not even drink when I got back and that is a plus for me. Shawn went shopping while I was there. I like when I can count his change and know he is doing something for himself. He is sleep and that girl he is with my grandchildren clowned with the bus driver after we left from seeing you.

These kids are bad. They woke me up

at 5 a.m. talking about the bus was

coming back up there. I am trying to

get Shawn and apartment, but I worry

about him being alone and having a

house full of people. I loved being

there and being able to be with you

made me happy. It filled the beer spot

that I could not wait to get home to

Happiness, that is what I need in my

life. Happy is what I am right now.

God loves me and shows me the way

when I get lost. He gives me direction

to go on. Do not worry because when

money come, I am going to get you

out of there if I have to spend every
dime of it. I realize how much you
need me to be strong. I am tired of
broken promises and wishful thinking.
I have to do this, that is why I will go
to the doctor so I can get stronger.
Well I am going in here with these
kids, they are quiet which means they
are doing something. Thinking of you.
Love Mom

A letter she wrote me dated March 23, 1998

Hi Poo. How are you doing? Find I
hope and pray. Well things out here
are not as well as I expected but ain't

nothing to be unexpected here. I got

your letter and book and boy you are

too damn smart to be there. I cannot

understand so many things in life, but

I have decided to deal with whatever.

I will be okay, please stop worrying

about me. I have always taken care of

myself and others for that matter. I

went to the laundromat and cleaned

my house. I do not want to go to the

hospital, but you have to realize the

pain and pressure I am under. I could

never leave my kids knowing they

were going through something.

Shawn claims that he do not need me,

but who else does he have? I want my baby home because he is not taking care of himself out there on that heroin, at least here I know I can watch him. I do not feel sorry for myself; I feel sorry for my children deep inside of me. I cannot do nothing but be patient and let God do His work. Only He knows how much I can take or judge me for that matter. I guess these are the prices that I pay for love. I might go to Reverend Banks church. I love you and there is no doubt in mama mind that God will send you home. God knows how much I need you here with me. Please understand me and most of all I know I am hard to deal with at times, but I promise you I will take better care of myself because I do not ever want to leave my kids or grandchildren. Just trust me to do the right things, I will. I am proud of you. You are too smart to be there baby hold on; help is on the way and believing in God is the best thing anybody can do in this world because there is no one else. Take care of yourself.

Loving you forever

Mom

A letter she wrote me dated

September 25, 1998

Hi, Poo. I went to Aunt Martha

funeral today and she had a nice

homecoming. Out here it is bad. We

are just living from day to day. I know

Shawn needs to get out of the house

sometimes and he needs people to

assist him. I do not think family is

treating him fair. I know he is a hand

full, but what do they expect from a

child of mine. I am sorry things are

not working out for me but like I said,

God here and He may not give me

what I want but He will always

provide me with what I need and be right on time. It is not looking good right now, but I refuse to give up. Tomorrow is not promised therefore you do not know what it will bring. I am so proud of you. I do not understand why you keep getting in trouble and I hope you will listen to me. I need you here. If I die tonight, all I can think about is who is going to help Shawn? I have not seen days like this in a long time, but I guess until God is ready to let us back in, this is how it will be. Do not be hard on your sister, she has a long way to go before she understands that I will never let her down and God knows I will never tell her anything wrong and the day will come when she will say she wish she had listened to me. Bobby it took me a long time to start over after the house burned down, but if you could see what I have gotten since then, you would not believe that I was in a fire. And that is a blessing. Do not worry, I know that if there is a will, there is a way. God will work it out in time, He always will be there. I will write in a couple of days to let you know what happens at court and where I will move. You just stay out of trouble, be strong, and keep your head above the water. It will be alright. Aunt Martha had a beautiful homecoming. It was a nice funeral. I hope that my mama be okay because she had just got back from her brother funeral out of town and I just feel like it is taking a toil on her. It is like I can see the pain she is holding inside. Nothing hurts more than pain inside of someone. My husband has not been doing drugs and I am proud of him and pray that God keep him strong. Even though he is broke, I think he can change and be a better person without it because he realizes things are not right and he see what is surrounding him and I like that. Please do not worry, it will be alright, and God will work it out. You will hear from me soon, so pray for us, we love you and mama will see her baby. Take care of yourself and stay out of trouble. I will always love you and hold you close to my heart.

Love mom

P.S. God is on our side and it is never too late to change or turn things around in life. Write soon. I need to hear from you.

~In Her Own Words: "A Kind Mother To Her Undeserving Kids"~

Chapter 23

Letters that my mother wrote me: A letter she wrote me dated May 4, 1998

Hi Poo. How are you doing? Fine, I hope. I need you to see if all of the kids are on your visiting list. Have you heard from your dad? I am still praying that God find it within His heart to give you back to me. I love you and always will. I am sorry for getting mad at you for looking like your father. He just hasn't been fair to me where my kids are concerned. It is not your fault. Nothing is happening out here, I am still looking for a house we can stay in. I do not like where we stay now. Everybody is okay here. I have not heard from your grandmother in a while, but she is okay, I guess. I am really looking forward to being there on Mother's Day with you. There is not a day that goes by that I do not think and want you home. I have a life, but I feel empty inside without my child and sometimes I wonder if you ever understand. This is not easy for me to accept with all that has happened with me and my kids. I hope you realize the pain that I endure and being strong is the only way for me to survive. Bobby Brown is sending you three books of stamps. Let me know when I can come up there. Boy I miss you. You are looking good boy. I saw the picture that you sent Shawn. Where is mine? I did not know it was here because I did not want to read his mail. They took Nicole kids; they are in a foster home. I feel sorry for her. Please write me and let me know what is going on in your life. I am worried about you. I will finish this letter later. 5/8/98 – Hi, I am finishing up this letter today. Sorry it took so long. Also, I got a Mother's Day card from you. Thank you. Why you did not send mama some money? You have always been cheap. I love you and always will. Call home.

I love you, Mom

A letter she wrote me dated June 27, 1998

Hi Poo. I was sitting here thinking about you and decided that writing was best. I love you and I do not know if you ever thought of what might have been if you were here, but sometimes I thank God for doing what was best, without knowing His reason cause living the life of not knowing can really hurt. Nothing is happening out here. I ask God to give you a break and send you home soon. I believe He is going to send you home soon. You are going to be okay. You know Shawn play that song "DEAR MAMA" for me every day. Every time I hear that song, nothing can touch the love I have for you. I miss you so much and did not realize the pain that you all have and still causes me inside. I also need you to stay out of trouble so I can get Shwn up because Shawn cannot fill your shoes and I think you are the only one that can make him see that cause God only knows the pain he is feeling. The fact that he cannot walk hurts me more than any pain I have ever endured and believe me when he got shot, that was pain. God spared his life. I know for a fact that only God can judge me. Michael, I am still made at him about what happened with his girlfriend, but I cannot stop loving him and being his mother.

Your sister is crazy in love. I have her kids and I wonder if she is okay. She do not realize what she is doing to these kids. I wish Dee would come home cause his son needs him. I have not heard from her in a few days; I wish she would come home. She said it is not enough room. I will make another room rather than to have to worry about her the way that I have been. My husband needs to go to the hospital. That heroin is eating holes through him and he will not stop. He is a good provider and he takes care of me, but he has got it all wrong because he should have been rich by now. All of your aunties and uncles are just being their same old selves. My mother is getting around and she stopped drinking, and she is looking good. Bobby I am tired of talking about family. I am not perfect myself. Just stay out of trouble long enough for me to see my child. I know it is not easy, but you made that bed. Do not stop me from sharing this pain with you; I need to see you. How are your criminal appeals going? When are you coming back for court? God, after Keeda get straightened up, I know her and Michael is going to make it in this world. Me and Shawn and my grandchildren are moving up there near the prison if this will make it easier for you? I want to be a part of your life and see you every time. Help me help you. I have these kids for the weekend, they are a mess. I need your help with Shawn because believe me, after me, he is going to be lost. He needs to see you like I do even though you made me too mad. I love you and do not worry about it because I am the mama. Boy you are 19 years of my heart, loving, and reasons to keep

going. Come on and straighten up so

you can come home. God's will be

done. Boy I am sitting here looking at

your picture, but I put it in a frame.

Send me some more. Have you heard

from Dee, Stacy, or Tracy? Your

nephew can be somebody, but he

needs a father figure to achieve what

is rightfully his. Guess what? A

library is on the corner. What do you

want me to look for? I am smart once

I get started. I got a brochure about

praying and it made sense. I am going

to copy it for you. My anniversary is

July 23rd. I might get a typewriter and sewing machine so I can make my grandchildren some clothes. Shawn is broke now, but he will be okay as long as I got breath in my body. Everybody is different. I will always love mine. I had five kids and never missed a day loving them. Ya'll love is important to me. You know I love raising my grandchildren. I have to watch them close. I know I will never be perfect, but God gave me you all for a reason. I respect the fact that I am not alone in this world. Poo life is worth it. God trusted me to raise ya'll, not to tell ya'll what to do, but I have not accepted that, I am sorry. I cannot. It is like when you left a part of me is gone. I have tried to handle this but cannot. When I drink, I lose it because deep inside the pain is more than I can stand. Your sister came and took her kids and I feel she is wrong because I worry about her so much and have to worry about my grandchildren. God even knows I do not deserve the pain that I am feeling. Shawn gave me a gold bracelet and said, "I love you mama." Do not ever think that God will not test you. I have learned the hard way. When you do not have money, nobody knows you. You will be surprised of your friends and the people who say, "I care." I am going to live until I die. It hurts when you due for a cry and cannot get it. I love you and we will make it through this together.

Love always and forever

Mom

A letter she wrote me dated July 9, 1998

Hi Poo. I got your letter and I am pleased that you are staying out of trouble. I made up my mind. I am moving up there whenever you go back to court. We can and will do this time together. I figure if I was closer it would be easier on you. Do not worry, you will never be without me. God will give us the strength to make it through this. I miss you too. About your cellmates whose mothers are deceased, I feel their pain. It is hard and there are some cruel people in this world. Do you want me to try and write the judge again and reason with her about my child? I need you here with me. It will not be much longer, I hope.

Love always

Mom

A letter she wrote me dated August 26, 1998

Dear Bobby,

I hope you noticed how this letter is written; mama is trying to type. I love you. How are you doing? Oh, and I hope you are staying out of trouble. When will you be back for court? Do not worry, I will be up there soon. I know you worry about me, but I will be okay. I am very proud of you and keep up the good work. I am going to put your G.E.D. and these poems you wrote in a frame. Things are pretty

much the same as when you left

except it has gotten harder. Do not get

in any more trouble. I need you here.

Did you talk to your caseworker about

who your judge is going to be? Let

me know so I can write him a letter as

soon as possible letting him know

how much I need you home. I cannot

begin to tell you how much I miss you

and need you here with me and

Shawn. I believe help is on the way.

We just have to hold on to each other

as well as God because only he can

help us be right. We cannot go

through this life without God. I

wonder everyday about tomorrow,

then when I see in the Bible that

tomorrow is not promised, it hurts

when you do not know. I cannot

understand why things go the way

they do in life, but everything happens

for a reason and only God knows. I

love and miss you. Well I will be

closing for now but wanted you to

know what I was up to besides in my

kids business if you let them tell it.

Do not forget how proud you have

made me okay. Kim brought you a lot

of books over here. I will send them soon.

Love Mom

A letter she wrote me dated August 30, 1998

How are you doing? Well I was sitting here thinking about you and wondering what you are doing? I hope you are staying out of trouble and working on your appeals. I also hope THAT YOU ARE DOING WHATEVER IS RIGHT and using your head so you will be home. I hope you listen for a chance. I only want what is best for you. I miss and need you here more than you know.

Believe me, life out here is hard. I am

worried about everything as usual. I

know how smart you are so do not let

me down. They cut my check off this

month and I do not know how I am

going to pay the bills. It seems like I

would have learned by now, but I

keep hoping for a change. I am trying

to think clearly and cannot even do

that right. I pray that I get lucky and

get a job this week. I know what I

have to do to hold things together for

me and Shawn. It is hard out here, but

I realize everybody has their own

problems. I refuse to be the burden nor let Shawn be one. I am going to do the best that I can to keep the phone on, but right now I need a place to stay. I hope you understand why I said, "I need you now." Because I know you will not let me down and can help. I believe if you were here Shawn would be walking. He listens to you when he will not pay me any attention. Well I will be closing now. Going to get the Sunday paper looking for a job this week so I can move as soon as possible and find something that I can afford. I hope you understand what I am saying. I guess there are a lot of things a person has to do just to get by and stay out of trouble. Stay out of trouble and be good.

Love

Mom

A letter she wrote me dated September 30, 1998

Hi Poo. I received your letter today and as always, very happy to hear from you. Shawn is in jail and I am unable to help again. They said he will get out. I haven't found a house yet but I'm still looking. I am packed, went to court and they gave me until

October 15th to be out of this house.

I'm so proud of you and hope you are

okay. Keeda brought the kids back

over here. Uncle Joe came over here

to see Shawn. My husband is still

clean, and I am proud of him. He has

gone back to work and is trying to

help me get a house. Bobby, I love

you and can't wait until you come

back to court. I pray for the best every

day. Satan knows how to work on me

because every time I do right and go

by the book, things do not work out

right, but when I do wrong things are

fine. Why is that? Mama is scared but I know what I have to do. I could not live with myself not knowing where Shawn is. I miss Shawn. I feel so alone in here. I guess by me never being alone is bothering me because I came from a big family and somebody was always home. I have to learn that this day would come when I have to do it alone. I keep saying that I am ready to do it alone but that be that beer talking because I feel like I am losing my mind. Your letters are getting better every time you write. Believe it or not, mama can feel your pain. I know you don't want me to worry. I hope I find a house by the 15th so I will not have to keep moving this heavy furniture. Well I am just writing because I promised you that I would write when I came from court. Please take care of yourself and hopefully the next letter will say everything that I have prayed for. And stop saying you are going to make me proud of you. I am already proud of you and love, need, and want you forever. I don't care if you're right or wrong. God gave me you and I'm just sorry for not being able to raise you the right way. I am not blaming myself; I am just wondering what I could have done different okay. I really like the poems that you send me. You really made my day with the G.E.D. I don't even have one of those; you go boy! Well I'll close for now. Stay out of trouble.

Love

Mom

A letter she wrote me dated November 1, 1998

Hey Poo,

How are you doing? Fine, I hope. I have not been at my best lately.

Today is Shawn birthday and he is still over my sister Virginia house until I get the house ready; it still needs work. I hope you stay out of trouble. I am staying over Pookie house until I get the house ready. Please take care of yourself. How much longer before you go back to court? It is taking a long time for you to tell me. Have you talked to Keeda? Don't forget to call Nicole. I hope things work out for me. It took a long time, but I finally got a house to where I do not and will not have to do without. It feels great. Bobby Brown is taking care of me. You have to get a job because I have to get money to help him out. Well I am going over Virginia house to spend time with Shawn and you will call while I am there. Please stay out of trouble and keep your head up and God will bring you home soon. I have to hold on to that and will not lose faith. I love you.

A letter she wrote me dated

January 4, 1999

Hey Poo. I just received your letter and picture today and is very proud of you. I have always said you are going to be somebody that I can truly say tried to make me happy in life. I am

having every roadblock there is with

this house and I know it's going to be

awhile because there's still a lot of

work to be done. I really have a

problem with the fact that this day

would come that I would no longer

have babies, and nothing lasts forever.

I haven't gotten past that yet. I did do

my best even though it could have

been better. Thanks for keeping me

strong. I'll never stop loving you and

just waiting on your return. I'm so

proud of you and deep in my heart I

know it's going to be alright. Stay out

of trouble. Keep your head above water and you'll be okay. Mama is proud of you and will always be by your side. Thanks for loving me. Happy 20th Birthday!

Love always & forever

Mom

A letter she wrote me dated August 13, 1999

Hi Poo. Miesha is staying with me for the summer. She is keeping granny strong. I can't let Shawn know how much I miss him. I have to get used to the fact that Shawn is not a baby anymore. I am proud of him getting his own and trying to pay the bills, but

I miss him being here with me or

never thought he would move out.

Bobby there is no place like home.

Don't give up, tomorrow makes a

difference and that better day is worth

waiting for we will never let this

corrupted world nor the people in it

get the best of us. Our love is real, and

God is on our side. You will be home,

be strong and use your mind. Be

careful and stay away from trouble.

You are trying to come home. Don't

ever think that you will not win

because you will. You have to help

the people on the outside. What happened to you the day you were sentenced is serious. I know it is hard on you, but you chose this by not listening. Think about what I have said in this letter. I'll always love you and be here for you.

Love always

Mom

A letter she wrote me dated

September 4, 1999

Hey Poo. I got your letter today and as always happy when I hear from you. My children is what keeps me going. I just pray that you are

listening to me. The pain is intense
sometimes, but I deal with it. I realize
it is rough and undermining, not to
mention the pain. I can understand
because mama knows pain, especially
yours. I've been there and the feelings
of hoping hurts. Don't think I don't
understand how hard it is there for
you and being strong is the best part.
I'm going to see you have and using
that sense that I know you have to
help someone else in need. I am
waiting for Keeda because we are
supposed to go shopping and
spending some time together. Shawn

and his wife are downstairs. I hope
they are getting along. I am so proud
of Shawn because he have his own
and a wife. I know you have wisdom,
sorrows, and regrets so use it. I need
you home. Bobby please believe that
freedom is not as far as it has been.
Baby we all cry, there's nothing
wrong with it, sometimes that is all a
person can do. 9/6/99 – Hi Poo.
Keeda just left. She came over so I
could cook her holiday food. I went
over Linda house earlier and got my
mama. I hate when someone hurt my
mother feelings. I can't stand to see

mine hurt. Have you heard from your daddy? I miss you so much. Don't sit back and dwell on the past unless it is something good. Nicole got her kids back. I went and bought her kids some shoes because she didn't have any money and I felt sorry for them because Nicole can't take care of them. They haven't started school yet, but I pray she put them in soon because I got the funds to get what they need.

9/10/99 – I wish I could begin to tell you all the pain that I have endured in life sometimes it wasn't even about me or my kids, but I've grown past

that and promised myself that I will

never look back again. It hurts to

know that the people you love hurts

you and can more than anyone else. I

will always be here for you. It seemed

like the older you all became, the

weaker my heart got instead of my

mind, ya'll now lay on my heart. But I

love every minute of it. Bobby, I

raised you all alone and did the best I

knew how then. I am not sorry for that

because I did a damn good job and

deserve a pat on the back. Everything

I did was out of love and concern. I

wish it could have been better, but I was living in the real world. I can't wait until you get your visit. Seeing you is important to me. I just hate that when visiting hours is over, you can't leave with me, but the time will come when I will not have to be concerned with that because you will be home. Just be strong and don't give up. I love you. I have made a lot of mistakes in life, but having my children was not one of them. I love you.

Mom

A letter she wrote me dated

October 20, 1999

Hey Poo. How are you doing? I know
my kids think I'm always in their
business, but you all are my business
and God I pray for the day that you all
realize whatever I do is out of love for
you all. Hold on, I love you and stay
out of trouble. Your sister left her
boyfriend and she blames me, but I
will do it again because I love her and
my grandchildren more than I love
myself, one day she will see that. I am
just afraid I will not be here when my
children realize how deep my love is

for them. I read your poems over and over sometimes hoping and praying that tomorrow brings a better day. When I do move, I am taking Shawn home so I know he will be okay and I will watch him like I promised God for letting my child live when the doctors did not know if he would wake up out of his coma. I will never forget that.

Love

Mom

A letter she wrote me dated

November 6, 1999

Hey Poo. Mom was happy to receive your letter. It made my day a little easier. The past, no we can't forget it but can put it behind us. God knows it will happen; trust and faith is all we need. Don't ever give up. I do not like writing you bad news knowing there is nothing that you can do about it but I believe in my heart that letting you know what's happening out here helps. Mama is waiting for your call. It's really hard for me to accept that fact that somebody other than me is bossing my child. I worry more than a normal person. I guess as long as I have children in this world, I will be worried. Baby I feel you when you hurt, I hurt. I know when something is wrong. I would not trade you for the world or the best. My heart aches continuously for my children. All I want is for all us with my grandchildren to stick together. I really get sick around the holidays. I know what the cause is; it's going to be that way until we are all together. Mama is proud of you and always will be.

Love always

Mom

A letter she wrote me dated

November 11, 1999

Hi Poo,

I am sitting thinking about you and

why you haven't called? I need to

hear your voice. Did Shawn send you

the pictures that he took on his

birthday? He bought a car. Keeda

moved into her apartment. I haven't

seen her in a week. She'll pop up. I

don't want to go looking for her

because she will get upset and say that

I'm in her business and to get a life,

not even thinking that she is my life.

Bobby I was going through my box

and going over those legal papers

about what happened at your

sentencing hearing and it is as plain as

day that my child did not disrespect

his mother. Can't we use that against

the judge since she lied? I believe in

not giving u on hopes and dreams. I

realize how hard it is for you but if

there is a will, there is a way and we

will find it. Just be strong because I

know you are a fighter and don't

believe in giving up because you got

that from me. Don't forget about these

court papers because I find a lot of fault in the judge and she should not be allowed to talk to people like that. That judge, Evelyn Baker, hurt my feelings because she lied on my child. But it is okay. My kids love me but have a hard time showing it with good reason. I love you.

A letter she wrote me dated November 26, 1999

Hey Poo. I love you. I was so happy when I heard your voice last night. Thank God. I miss you. I was so thankful yesterday just hearing your voice made mama happy. I keep on worrying about everything but myself. Your sister and sister-in-law hung out with me last night for Thanksgiving. Your sister made me feel special telling me how much she loves me, just don't like me in her business, but she'll understand that she is my business and she ain't grown to me. To me she is my missy baby girl, so she wasting her time telling me that she is grown. I might pick my mama up today to spend some time with Shawn so she can cook. That makes her happy once in a while. She miss my father. I love you and I want my baby home more than anything else in the world right now and God knows that. Please stay away from trouble and people that cause you to get in trouble. Keep your head up. I love you.

Mom

A letter she wrote me dated December 3, 1999

Hi Poo,

Well as usual mama was happy to hear from you. I haven't and wouldn't ever turn my back on ya'll for anyone or anything because I love ya'll more. I know that my children love me, but

I've always asked ya'll to stick
together. I wish my children will
realize that I deserve a life too, but I
also refuse not to have them in it. I
don't want my husband to leave, but
my family, most of all my children,
come first even if that means hurting
myself. I worried that every time I get
through something with one of you
all, believe me the next one is in line
to start worrying me all over again.
Sometimes being strong is my only
defense when it comes to you all.
Would you please talk to your
brothers and sister because ya'll

staying together is very important to me. My hope is that all my grandchildren stick together. Saying that he is a grown man is Shawn favorite words, but I know my kids need me. But if he would just listen and just try it mom way one time, I promise he would see the light. I love you all more than self and that is a lot of love to give away unconditionally. Don't worry it will be okay. Mama know how to take care of self and her children. I don't worry about the outcome because I know that even if I was wrong, just knowing that I did all

I could do to help my children means a lot to me. When I get real mad knowing that I can't win, I pray and think about what I want to change. Believe me it works instead of reacting and stooping down to someone else level. Stay out of trouble.

Love Mom

A letter she wrote me dated December 17, 1999

Hey Poo,

Mama got your letter and always happy to hear from you. I am sorry that I missed your call. Miesha was so excited about the letter that you wrote her until I started to cry. Bobby about the family sticking together, that is all that mama really ever asked of her children. Shawn bought Muffin some shoes, but I am still worried about him but thankful for the rest at night because it's heavy on me out here. Bobby do not beat up on yourself for not understanding how hard it was for me. Thank you. Besides your brothers and sister still have to grow or have not stopped to think yet. Maybe they have to get in a position in order for them to think that far. As for Nicole, I pray that she hurry up and straighten

out her life because those kids need

her and she should care more for

herself and them after living the life

she lived, but I guess it's going to take

more than she realize. I just pray that

it don't be too late. She can't see the

life that she lived and putting her

daughters through the same thing isn't

fair. Therefore, I do not know what

else to do to help them. You know I

would let them live with me and try to

help them, but my husband is not

having it because he feels like people

be taking advantage of me. I still try

to help. I be sneaking given them
money for food and I think my
husband would have a fit if he found
out. I am getting older, but my heart is
big and strong, and I will help
anybody with all that I got. If I knew
back then the things I know now,
baby life would be a lot different for
me. Your nephew is giving your sister
a fit by staying in trouble. I told her
this day would come but it's awful
early at his age so therefore I have to
step in and help her before he gets
completely out of hand. My husband
family have never accepted me due to

the fact that he married with all of my children and he was nobody daddy. In a way I understand, but they have to realize that he loves me and understand the life he was living and that is why I accept the tree people that my kids is involved with now. So therefore, I will be on the outside looking in until I die because I love my children enough to know that I can't stand to bare to lost them because I didn't accept what they wanted. Yes, that hurts bad but the truth feels better. There are going to be many things that they do that I do not approve of, but if they are happy, what can I say? I dislike when I am put in a situation in which I have to choose between my husband and kids and that is what I mean when I say I can't win for losing. You can't make nobody do nothing but hope and pray for change, and sometimes that takes a lifetime but anything worth having is worth waiting for. My marriage is important to me. I am not getting any younger. Just wanting to feel young and live my life to the fullest. My kids could always depend on mama to make sure that they will never go

hungry because I will keep
something, and my grandchildren
never have to worry about being
hungry when granny is around and
that feels good. Miesha is very smart
and just seeing and growing up
around here makes her want more in
life. She wants to be a judge when she
gets older. These kids are amazing.
They keep me smiling when I am sad
usually. I get my grandkids; they are
guaranteed happiness for me. I am
sleepy but walking the floor waiting
on Shawn to pull up in his car so I can
go to sleep 12/18/99 – Mama was

very happy to hear your voice

yesterday, made me happy. Keeda

dropped the kids off and you know

they are driving me. I am doing well

except I am worried about all of you

as usual. I never really realized what

raising kids was about until Miesha

came along and I had to start all over.

I am overwhelmed with your

understanding. The fact that you have

grown up is enough for me. I pray that

my children will see what is going on

and how hard it is to have to do it

alone all my life. I only wanted the

best or make well do for you all.

Nobody helped me but the government welfare system and giving me a check to try and stretch farther than it could go just to make ends meet. I wish you were here. I don't understand why it took this for you to realize what I have been through in life, but I guess in time I will get the answer. I care what the next person feels in life and believe me, it's no fun. Bobby sometimes raising a family alone isn't easy from the start, but what choice do a person that wants to make it have? Mom could write a book on life and the repercussion it causes. I am trying to give my grandchildren everything that you all did not have, trying to understand them like I should have understood you all. In other words, God has given me another chance, but only this time I have to do it His way. That is the only way for real, but I am just learning to know God and that He cares whatever the problem may be. I have got to trust God and believe that a change gonna come. Sometimes your way is not the right way. We all need help and somebody and that's no secret. Please take care of yourself.

A letter she wrote me dated

December 11, 1999

Hey Poo,

I took the kids to go get the toys that

you sent them for Christmas. They

gave your mother a fit. Everybody is

fine and sends you their love. I love

you. It is now Sunday afternoon and I

just finished wrapping the gifts for

grannies. I can't wait to come up there

and see you; mama miss her baby. It

is the holidays and it hurts that you

are not here. Mama is going to take

some pictures of your father for you

one day. I really wouldn't care if I

ever saw that man again. Understand why I feel this way. Nicole is back. It's the holidays and I am the only one that she can turn to. You know she burns all of her bridges everywhere else she goes and now her kids don't have toys, but like always, I got them covered. Those were some nice gifts that you got for the kids. Thank you. Stay away from trouble and quit learning the hard way Poo. Trouble is easy to get into, but hard to get out of. We all love and miss you dearly.

Love

Mom

A letter she wrote me dated

January 7, 2000

Hey Poo,

Mama got your letter today and was

very happy to hear from you.

Everybody is fine. I am just waiting to

see my child. I love you boy. Miesha

birthday is Monday. I decided to just

give them ice cream and cake. I can't

wait to give you her letter. She be so

excited when she receives a letter

from you. Shawn helped her read it.

Bobby don't worry about mom; I'll be

alright. Besides, quitting isn't in me. I

love you and glad you are beginning

to understand me. I hate the way that you have had to learn about your mother's struggle in life. Be thankful and hold on. God will answer my prayer. I love you. Stay strong and out of trouble Mr. Bostic.

Love always

Mom

A letter she wrote me dated

February 2, 2000

Hey Poo,

Mama had a rough day. Nicole, Mike, and Keeda kids are here. My husband and I are arguing over why I got all these kids. He thinks that everybody walks over me. He is always

complaining about me babysitting

other people's kids. I always felt that

without my kids, there is no me, no

matter what. I love and miss you.

Have to run, take care of yourself and

stay out of trouble.

Love

Mom

A letter she wrote me dated March

11, 2000

Hey Bobby,

I woke up happy. Mama was so glad

to see you boy. You looking good. I

pray this will be over soon, most of all

I get my child back. These pictures
are the bomb. I'll keep up with them.
I'll be up for the food day with the
kids. And stop trying to tell me what
to do. I love you and mind your
business.

Mom

**A letter she wrote me dated March
25, 2000**

Hey Poo,

Mom was just sitting here watching
her surroundings and please believe
they don't look good. It hurts coming
there knowing that it is not to pick
you up. I was really happy yesterday

because I promised those kids that they would see their uncle soon. They was so happy until I flipped out. I couldn't sleep last night due to the thought of you being there. I pray that God come through for my sake. I love you. You are a kid that has learned his lesson. That's all I ask that judge to see, but she couldn't even give us that. You look just like your daddy and I hate that man, but I'll never take that out on you. I am going to get back up there soon. Take care of yourself.

Love always, Mom

A letter she wrote me dated April 7, 2000

I haven't wrote because I have had these kids since we left from up there and they are wearing me out. Kim (cousin) is here. Her and Lauretta (auntie) and mama all came over here last night and stayed awhile just talking, laughing, and having a good time. I wish you were here. I put your pictures in an album in my purse, so you go everywhere I go, keeping an eye on you and remember the goodness that lies upon your heart. Your brother said that he is getting married next year, but he still has four girlfriends. Now you tell me. I've always told ya'll to stay together no matter what. I refuse to give up. I might give out, but not up. Hope that my children will listen or realize that one day you all will be telling your own kids that mama was right, or mama told me this or that. God is my witness that I have nothing but love for you all. I don't regret a day for having you all even with all the ups and downs. God I wouldn't trade my kids for the world if I had a chance I would choose you all because there were times when you all have made me feel unworthy and other times when you all have made me feel like I am the best mother that a kid could have. I'm sorry you had to learn the hard way but baby I am thankful because there are many mothers that will not see their child again. Stay strong and out of trouble, you can do it. What the courts have did with you ain't the answer, the details aren't even right. That is why you have to keep working on it so you can get home with family where you belong. Remember it's never too late and don't give up. I'm lucky because at least God spared you and Shawn life letting me know there's a chance for better things to happen for all of us. Sweetheart you are very smart and making something out of your life is the right thing to do. I am proud of you anyway. All through my childhood, I saw brothers and sisters fighting each other, that's why I get upset when you all argue at each other. I would go off to myself and drink and cry because all I ever wanted was you to stick together. Bobby the only way you can repay is by coming home okay, so correct

yourself. I'm very proud of you

period. You are my child no matter

what. Besides, I probably wouldn't

still be living if it were not for you all.

You don't owe me nothing. That's

what mom is for. I'll always be there

through the good and the bad. I love

me enough to cover that wind that I

think may come in. my heart pumps

happiness baby that mama know is

coming. I just hope that I don't be

depressed and it slides right by me.

Bobby smile. You are crazy, baby

you'll always be on my nerves and I

guess I wouldn't have it no other way. You are a miracle boy because you are my child. I have to be strong for all of us. You all have made me a strong mother and do not realize how lucky I am for you all. Mama just start cooking and I have a money problem because I am broke. This bill is too high, and I will never get a bill like this again. I hope I make a difference as far as my grannies are concerned because things just aren't right out here. Everybody miss you.

Love Mom.

A letter my sister wrote me dated

May 29, 2000

Bobby,

I'll always love you....

Bobby, I know you are upset with me.

First of all, I would like to say I am

sorry. I also know you know what's

going on with mom and me. I want

you to know it is hurting me. But

mom has to realize I had my son Boo-

Man. Boo-Man is my child. She has

to let me raise my family. Bobby I am

trying my best to raise my kids the

right way. If I don't, who is? It's time

for mom to let go and let me raise my

family. She raised me and now it is time for me to raise mine.

Love

Keeda

A letter my mother wrote me dated July 15, 2000

Hey Poo,

Willie is dead and the family went to the funeral Friday. He was shot by some boy who was trying to take his car for the wheels. I am sending you the clipping from the newspaper. His mother Deloris is really strong because I pray God take me first. I love my kids too much and wouldn't want to go on without either of you. Shawn has to go to court because they are putting him out of his house. I will make sure that he has a roof over his head though. I am afraid for him. One of his friends got shot down there. I broke my camera today, but I will buy another one tomorrow. I love sending pictures and I can imagine how it is to see your loved ones. Pictures are worth a thousand words sometimes. I wish I didn't have both hands full, but I do, and it is hard out here. I got your letter today and you sure know how to cheer mom up. Thank you. I love you and most of all miss you. God has been good to me; at least you are not dead baby. I know that worrying does not help but baby that's all mama know and is an expert at doing it. I've learned to be prepared for whatever even though it scares me sometimes. Deloris is in so much pain. She has lost two sons, her oldest and her baby. God had lifted a burden off of her for whatever reason He chose to. That's the only way. 7/18/2000 – I can't help but worry. God knows that I try not to. Things are not working out for me out here, but all I can do is hold on

and hope for a better day. When
tomorrow comes, it only gets worse. I
feel so alone out here trying to raise
Miesha. It's like starting all over with
you all. I raised you all alone. Thanks
for understanding me in ways that
nobody else does. I love you. I will
write later, hopefully with better news
and better things to say. I refuse to
give up on anything worth fighting for
and my husband and kids mean
everything to me. Here is a clipping
about the high prices they charge
prisoners to use the telephone. They
do charge too much for you all to call

home making it hard on the people

who have to pay the bills, which is not

fair. I am worried about all of you, my

bills, and my private life. I am looking

forward to Friday when we come to

see you. Seeing all of my kids

together is happiness that is

overwhelming me. I can't control it.

Love always

Mom

A letter she wrote me dated August

19, 2000

Hey Poo,

How are you doing? I pray that you

are staying out of trouble. Shawn has

10 days to move out of his apartment.

I am trying to find him a house

because Monday his time is up. I hope

he moves back home before I go back

to work. I can't stand to see them

setting my child out on the streets. He

is playing hard as usual. Have you

heard from your father? I am very

sick. I know smoking cigarettes has a

lot to do with whatever it is, but

mama hate hospitals and funerals. I

try to stay away from both of them. I

have nothing but love for my kids;

you all mean everything to me. When

you get this letter, call home. Stay out

of trouble.

Love always

Mom

A letter my mom wrote me dated

September 13, 2000

Hey Poo,

Mama is writing to let you know she

still sick and my leg is really hurting

on my birthday. Shawn will not listen.

I cannot get through to that child. I am

scared for him. He went back to the

hospital, but he refused to stay. Bobby

mama is really proud of you for

staying out of trouble. Most of all for

thanking me for bringing your nieces

and nephews up there. Your sister

said she will be up there soon. I love

and miss you a lot. Baby it is not that

mama don't want to talk there; it hurts

me just being there. I need and want

my child home. These kids are bad,

but I can't see myself without them.

Holding my head up is always my

way out. It is 12:40 p.m. and I just

came from getting the mail. Thanks

for the birthday cards. I knew you

would, I thought they would be late.

Guess what, they make me feel like a

Happy Birthday Girl. These cards are

worth more than gifts to me. I know I

haven't been the best, but I've always

loved and made a way for my

children. Some of the things that I

have done in life I was not proud of,

but God I'll do it again in a heartbeat

for my kids. I am so happy these cards

came. They made me feel happy

because I was down on my birthday,

but this afternoon feels like more

happiness will come my way today.

Thank you, baby. Mama cannot stand

to see you locked up, but I have to

deal with this. I haven't accepted it

yet because every day it gets harder

for me. Thanks for the cards. Mom will cherish them forever. I will be up there next month, but I am going to bring the kids. I might have to bring Miesha also because I do not have anybody to watch her. It feels like I had her. She is with us 24/7 except when she is at school, but I love her so much. It makes me feel young raising a child again. It's been a long time, but I will sacrifice whatever for her. I promise to make the best of the day and most of all thank God for allowing me to be here. Baby, mama will be happy when you get free.

Love always

Mom

A letter she wrote me dated

November 13, 2000

Hey Poo,

Mama is sorry for missing the visit, it

will not happen anymore anytime

soon, that is how much I love and

miss you. I was so proud of your

sister for coming up there to see you.

She really needed the break. Baby that

girl sat through my surgery the whole-

time crying, most of all showing me

love that I never thought she had.

Bobby, mama has cancer and it is real

bad. I will be okay because I am

strong in heart and soul. Besides, look

at all God has given me to live for. I

wish I would have realized that and

caught it in time, but that comes from

not going to the doctor. Mama has

never believed in that, but from now

on if I get a scar in me, I am running

to the hospital. I got my hip removed

and a nurse comes here every day

trying to teach me how to walk again,

but I don't like that either because

once mama taught a child how to do

something in life, it never forgot how

to do it. I'll be up in no time. The

cancer is pretty bad, and they didn't get it all out and still searching for where it is. I pray every night that God helps them find it before it's too late. Don't worry about me, mama was scared at first, but now I know these pills will keep me alive. I have to have them. They are so high, but I'll find the money before they get to put my life on hold. Keeda said you all had a good time on visits. Mama did not know that the world had so much pain in it, especially in one's body. I still can't walk but hold your head up; I'm a fighter and am really

trying. It hurts, but for the love of
ya'll I'll be fine. I am so proud of
your cousin Kim for flying right down
here worried about me and said she
remembered how painful it was for
my sister Carol. I was happy to see
her; it meant a lot to see my family
support me during that time because
God knows I was afraid. He didn't
allow me to be down. I feel so much
better at home. It is going to be hard
for a minute, but God will lighten this
heavy load. I love you, please don't
worry about me. I know for sure that
is a lot to ask. The medicine is very

high, and my husband just went and got it, but without mama would not survive too long. Bobby I did not know that a human being could experience so much pain until I experienced it myself. It is awful. I love you and miss you. Will write again tomorrow. 11/15/2000 – Hi Poo, mama just got a card and letter from you. Thanks. I love you. I know you were happy to see Keeda. Mama is just scared and in a lot of pain. But deep down I know I will be okay. I am very upset because I cannot take care of myself. Now I realize how

Shawn felt when he first came home.
It hurts so bad and the family is
showing me all love. They have really
been here for me but mama just like
that, she don't want nobody waiting
on me. Call me as soon as possible;
NEED TO TALK TO YOU. I am
hurting but will be okay. Keep your
head up. I love you.

Mom

**A letter my mother wrote me dated
November 20, 2000**

Hey Poo,

Mom received your letter today and
as always love to hear from you.

Don't worry about me smoking, I will

quit when I get ready, you stop

worrying me with that. I know I will

not be able to make the food visit on

the 6th, but I will do everything in my

power to be there on the 15th. I am

tired of pleading with your little

brother to do right. There are many

21-year-old boys that wish they had a

mother like me, but your brother does

not realize the love within me for him.

I have cancer and I am not going to let

it beat me as long as I am strong,

don't feel sorry nor give up. God will

hold my hand through this. I hate

being down and not being able to walk, but I've been trying to keep my spirits up and smile and even be walking on my walker. Keeda is showing me all love. I just hate that this had to happen to receive it from her. Fear is a person's biggest problem in life because it can hinder you. I can deal with this except that the insurance company been coming over and putting the icing on the cake. I just wonder what the doctor told the family. It is something that I don't know. I am sicker than the family is letting on. I can feel it, but sweetheart mama is going to make it. Sometimes you have to lose in order to win. I know this is a battle, but I am a good fighter and will be strong to the end. Don't worry. I thank God for letting me see the light before it becomes dark. I promise I will not give up; I might give out but not without a fight. I just pray the family will try to get you out the way they are planning my life. The doctor wants me back in the hospital, but I refuse because I know what is upsetting me and I feel like they want an experimental pig and it will not be me. The more upset I become, the worse the blood clot get, and they are traveling through my body on top of the cancer eating me up. Giving up is not on mom's list. Baby I look around here every day and have every reason in the world to be strong and loving every minute of it knowing how much I love my family. I will fight the world alone for you all. Don't ever forget that you all is my world and worth me living getting stronger every day.

11/21/2000 – Hey Poo, mom has slept since I left the hospital. I am in so much pain. See God has given me so much and that is why I am as worried about you as I was at first because it will be okay. Mama was scared but she has accepted the bad with the good. The pain is very intense now. I feel what I have heard a lot about. I am determined to win. Poo you are beautiful, I look at your pictures every day and ask God how could the smartest child that I had get himself into so much trouble. I could write an essay on the love that I have for my family. Growing up is rough and I know that it is hell in there. This world is cruel out here. Keeda is mad at me because she found me in pain, and I wouldn't let her take me to the hospital, but that was because I go to the doctor tomorrow. By she is really mad at mom. Said she can't stand to see me in pain. I understand. I'm proud of you and keep up the good work. I miss you Poo. My daughter comes over here before work every morning and checks on and takes care of me showing me all loving and understanding. My sickness has bought us closer. God knows what He is doing. I was reading a book yesterday, it said that worrying is not going to add another day to life, only take it away. God works at His pace, I realize that He is busy, that is why He gave us five senses. Sometimes you have to figure it out on your own, the path you choose is on you but not to worry, God will lead you the right way before it is over. It is up to you to choose the way. I went to the doctor and got the staples taken out. The doctor said to see how I respond to chemotherapy to find out his next step to treating my cancer. I am strong, mama will win this battle. I have never suffered so much pain. I know I suffered having kids, toothaches, but it hurts. I have heard people talk about the pain, but it is amazing that one could endure so much pain. I am trying to get pain and swelling out of my leg now so I can walk, stand long enough to do my work. Keeda and my husband cleans up the house, but not like I want it done. I hate filth. Hopefully by next week I will be back to my old self. I hate people waiting on me. I hope the chemo works to control the cancer because it is never going away, but it can help to prolong my life in the long run. I will write after I go to the doctor and let you know how that went. I am proud of you Poo, please stay out of trouble. Every one of us has to step up to the plate in life. Baby this is a cold world, well at least the people in it are. I feel like they railroaded you in that courtroom, right or wrong my child did not deserve what they gave him. Don't worry because God understands and will straighten this problem out in a matter of time. Keep your head up and call me, I miss you.

Mom

A letter my mother wrote me dated December 4, 2000

Hey Poo,

Your typing is really working out well. I love you with all my heart and if God speaking to me through you it is okay. Ever heard of the man that drowned and went to heaven? Well a car came by and tried to pull him from the water, he refused, then a man on a raft came along, he refused, last a helicopter dropped a rope down, he refused so he drowned. When he saw God, he asked why didn't you save me? I wait, God replied, I sent three

people and you didn't respond so I did
what was best for you. I haven't
stopped smoking, but I have slowed
down, meaning I am trying. Don't be
so hard on me, work with me. I will
quit and there is nothing that I would
not do for you all. They still haven't
found where the cancer started but
have to soon because is it steadily
spreading and eating me up. The
problem is that I hope that it do not
touch any more bones because that
means more operations and I refuse
another one. I asked God to show
them where the cancer is. Baby I

promise that I'll be alright. God is making sure that I fully understand what is going on and I am close to death I can't reach because God did not bring me this far to fail me now. He knows that I still have plenty to do here. I am strong and still live life to the fullest. I thank God every minute, he's never right there but always on time. I'm tired but refuse to give up and will not, mama got to fight back harder. I realize what you are saying about smoking and you are right, and I am quitting. It is going to be okay. Please help mama through this. It is important to me. Hey Poo, it's

Saturday 4:55 a.m. Mom is in a lot of

pain this morning. I can't take

medicine until 8 a.m. Do you know

that I still find myself hollering, I

want my mama, because I be in so

much pain. Mama promise I am

listening to you about smoking and

hopefully it will not be much longer

before I quit again. I got to tell you

that I am scared and do not feel like I

am getting better. Baby I want to walk

without pain, my body is so tired but

only in one leg. I tried taking a break

and doing nothing but thinking, I

can't. Whatever happens you all stay together and protect one another. Please call home and see about your mother. Mama is a fighter and I am going to help the doctors find this cancer. Mom wants to go to church, but do not have to because God hears you. He's coming when He feels it's time. Baby time stands still for no one except God, wasting it is not such a good idea. They say that a cancer patient will endure a lot of pain, but I have been in pain all my life. The happiest painful moment was giving life to you all. A day doesn't go by that I don't miss you. I knew that

cancer ran in the family and I should

have questioned if I had it when I was

warned, but mama is a strong person

and she only gets sick every now and

then and that only last four or five

days. I am so happy that you all are

grown, but then again, now I have to

learn when to let go because to me

you all will always be my babies in

heart, soul, and mind. The best

teacher in life is self. I ask God to

help me where I am weak because I

fully understand that I am just the

type of mother that just will not let go

of her kids. I received your letter today and was happy to hear from my baby. You are the smartest child that I got and that has never been a secret in our family. Shawn came up here and spent the night. I knew it, my baby feelings were hurt. I felt him down there, finally he came up here where he knows he is loved. I didn't say anything, but God I know when something is wrong with my children. I can feel it. I thank God for that instinct. Well today is the last of this letter. Keeda is getting on my nerves because she has the whole family worried about me. Call home and

check on mama, the letters are okay,

but your voice is better. Well mama is

closing but never will she close her

heart. Take care of yourself and call.

Keep your head up and I love and

miss you.

Mom

Ya'll Gone Miss Me

Ya'll gone miss me is what mama used to
say
Oh how I wish she was here today
I know things wouldn't be this way
I took her love for granted because I thought
she was here to stay

Everyone has to die
When death overtook my mother, I asked
God why
I figured that she would never go
That's why I wanted to know

I still wonder why she had to leave
For this reason, every day I grieve
What is life without my mother
To take her place there is no other

Mother I do miss you
Today your every word rings true
I was hardheaded and didn't want to listen

Now it's you that I'm missing

You told me that nobody would ever love
me the way you did
I remember hearing these words from you
ever since I was a kid
Although everything that you said I heard
I gave little attention to your caring word

Mother I am so sorry for not listening
I am sitting here wishing
Wishing that you were here with the family
Remembering your words when you said,
"Ya'll gone miss me"

~YA'LL GONE MISS ME~

Chapter 24

As long as mama was around, we always knew that we had someone on this earth who loved us. No matter what happened, she was always that soul that loved us unconditionally. Sometimes people never appreciate a good thing the way that they should until that thing or person is gone. We always took such statements from her in a nonchalant way because she had been telling us, "There is not one going to love ya'll like mama do." In a sense, we took her love for granted because we always figured that she would be around. But what happens when mama is not around? We always assumed that she would outlive all of us because of the fast lifestyles that we were living. We assumed that God would protect her because of her good nature and kind heart. Of course, we have seen her in pain and occasional sickness many times, but each time she regained her health and picked her spirits up and became even more stronger and vibrant than before. When I learned that my mother had cancer, I instantly assumed that she would overcome it in no time. For 21 years, I had witnessed her overcome all of her other battles internally as well as externally. She was made of mountains, so I never once imagined that her time was near.

Somewhere within my soul I assumed that I would die before my mother did. When she developed last stage cancer, I still would not accept the fact that my mama would die. I denied this until the last minute. It has been four months since she passed, but in the back of my mind, I still do not accept the fact that she is not here with us. I can't explain it, but she will always be here with me. I still hear her talking all of the time.

About six days from her departure, we spoke on the phone and she was giving me hints that she knew it was her time. Instead of hearing what she was trying to tell me, I was saying, "Mama it is never too late, you are going to be okay, you just need to quit smoking cigarettes and worrying so much." She just did not want to tell me if someone else was in the house, she would pass the phone to them or just change the subject. I would be getting on her nerves telling her to go to the hospital. Although my intentions were good, I should have listened to the message she was trying to send me. I did not and could not accept those words coming from my mama, so I pretended that I didn't hear them. In her own protective caring way, she listened to me and changed the subject to more happier things. I refused to accept any weakness coming from the strongest person I have ever known.

She told me about her having a grandchild on the way. She also shared some of her visions and dreams with me. I remember she told me she had a dream and saw Shawn walking and said that he could walk if he would really try. By telling me her dreams she knew that I would do everything in my power to make her dreams a reality. I must admit that my mother knew her kids even better than we knew ourselves. I remember she used to say, "Bobby I know you like a book."

This was absolutely the truth. She knew my moods and actions as if I were a well-studied book and she remembered the contents of the pages. Flipping through the pages she would tell me my own story but being blind in my rebellion I acted as if I couldn't read the words she was spelling out to me and it cost me dearly.

I now know what it means to truly miss someone. I know what it feels like to be truly full of regret and even tears can't cry away the pain. All of her kids really miss her. Regretting the countless times that I didn't listen, now her very words haunt me every day when she would say, "Boy one day you gonna wish that you had listened to me." I cannot turn back the hands of time, but I wish I could tell her how sorry I am for taking her through all of the things that I took her through. I know that she would tell me that there is no reason to be sorry. Knowing this still does not make it any easier for me. I know that I could have treated her a lot better. I ask myself why couldn't I see the big picture? Why couldn't I realize what I was taking her through and change my behavior? I know that she would not want me to carry this burden, but my conscience still haunts me on this. She told me that "when time is up it is up." These words are hard to accept when it comes from your mother. She was only 42 years old when she died of cancer, so of course I figured she had many more years to live. Every time I achieve something or accomplish a goal I always say, "I wish mama was here to see this." Even when I fail or make a mistake, I still wish she was here because she would not criticize, she would simply say, "It is going to be alright."

She always told us that she would never tell us wrong and wanted what was best for us. Even when we were rebellious, she kept on loving us every day anyway. I admit that we took her through too much and now it is time for us to go through some things on her behalf. Her kids can be anywhere in the world but when we think about her, we start crying because now that she is gone there is a void in our lives that can never be filled. I know that she does not want us to think of her in a sad way, she wants her children to be happy no matter what. She does not want us to live in regret for not listening to her, she just wants us to listen to her now. The things that hurts me the most is that we did not get a chance to show her how much we love and appreciate her. In the same way that many martyrs gave their lives for freedom, my mother labored, suffered, struggled, and took her last breath for her children. Now all so clearly, my sister, my brothers, and me remember when mama told us, "Mark my words,

ya'll gone miss me."

~MAMA'S GOING HOME~

Chapter 25

The final letter that my mother wrote me before she died:

Hey Poo,

I know you are worried about me. Thanks. I know I am sick, but I am also afraid because I know that nobody is going to put up with Shawn other than me. I want to be well but I already know what the doctors are trying to find and have been knowing it; just didn't want to hurt or worry anyone else. I try and do this myself all of the time, but when it don't work, the pain I feel inside is different. Please stay out of the lock up hole, help me help you. You are right, you can't begin to know what I feel inside and not to mention it feels like it ain't giving in. Guess what? I'm not giving up. The pain is intense. I've turned the other cheek so much in life until I just put them both out there at the same time to keep from being hurt after the fact. The truth is raising ya'll wasn't easy. It hurts so bad to look around and your kids are grown, and you can't do anything with them, now that's pain. I have cancer and have known it for a while and just don't talk about it because my kids need me. I've been told years ago to stop smoking and I didn't. before I die, I want a red brick house for my children to always be secure knowing they are taken care of means everything to me. Don't forget my white fencer okay? I want my kids to live forever. Well things is bad out here and I promised that I would not lie to you again about what is going on out here. They turned the lights off today, but don't worry I will have them back on tomorrow. Thanks for thinking that I deserve better, but what I deserve is you home. Hey Poo, it's another day. The lights are back on. Please be strong for me. I'll be alright. I just want this cancer to go away and allow me to fulfill my dreams and most of all for my children to stay together. I've convinced myself that I am okay. I thank God every day. Michael just called and said he'll go to the doctor with me and now I have to hid because I can't stand to see my child hurt. I already know what is wrong, I just want it to go away. I have never been scared of anything. I don't like what I am seeing. My kids are my world, I could just live in the world with my kids and their kids around me. I got to see my kids through this mean world. I know you all are grown but still my babies to me. I have some bad kids. Don't give up. I can't talk about how stubborn you are and hardheaded, don't change. I love you just the way you are. It's going to be okay. God forgives and don't forget. Only Satan forgets because he is busy. I wonder about in the beginning of the world when Noah built the boat, why didn't the people get on the boat? I would have got on the boat and took my kids with me. I don't mean to hurt you all. I am scared to leave you all in this mean world. If I go into the hospital, I will feel like I gave up. I can't accept the fact that I might not be here for my kids. I know that when time is up it is up. I just got a letter from you. Bobby please don't ask things of me that I can't promise. I go to church alone. And I needed this letter. I pray that God makes me well. He has never failed me throughout it all. That's why I wonder why I can't ask questions? Let me do the worrying you already have enough on you. Please try and understand. I know it's hard. God has always shown me the way when I get lost.

Every day He makes sure that I have something to keep going. He knows that I can't keep going like this, so why can't you all? Believe in yourself. I love you. Bobby, I have so much to do here, taking care of you all is first. Please try and understand and please stop asking me so many questions. I have my reason. I need answers. God blesses me every day. I do know that I can't give up. Like I said, I already know what's wrong, but I'm also scared. You think this is easy for me? God has forgiven me; I just haven't forgiven myself. I am

- 517 -

sorry, I just can't see ya'll hurting and God knows Shawn is hurting, but only Shawn can let God in to help him. Don't ya'll tear up my house. Keep it for ya'll kids to raise theirs in. I got to get this house fixed and in order, so much to do and nothing to do it with, that's what is killing me. I feel Shawn's pain, want to do it yourself but can't walk. He is used to getting up doing for himself and going about his business. Now to wonder and hope somebody help him. It hurts and I can feel his pain and it is tearing me apart. Okay I accept the fact that Shawn got shot. God spared his life and I am thankful, but where do I go from here? I got to keep going, refuse to give up. Bobby please listen, it's going to be okay, you will be home. Trust God, it will work out. I need to be at peace within myself. I close my eyes and see Shawn in that coma, not knowing I was even there, but I thank God when he woke up his first word was, "Mama." I'll never forget that day. He knew something had happened. I stayed there and when they told me Shawn couldn't walk, but when I settled down, I realized that he was alive and never say never. You'll never know, only God knows. Bobby your sister, brothers, and my husband knew that I was sick, but I never admitted it. So, whatever happened, don't blame them. I am trying to figure out how I can win. I am trying in a whole bunch of ways. I don't know how but learning is something that I have to do. Hold on. I love you. No more questions. I am fine okay.

Always here for you

Mom

P.S. Hold on, help is on the way. Don't give up. Bad kids, your mother know. Take care, Mama loves you. Don't forget my house. It's red with a white fence.

A great speaker once said that "there are some things, some dear, some things so precious, some things so eternally true, that they are worth dying for." Surely my mother felt that her kids and grandchildren were worth dying for and she died for us. When her physical body took its last breath, it departed, but she will always be in our hearts and her great spirit still shines on us.

God sent us many signs before she passed. Since He knew that it was time for her to go, He sent my older brother back home to live with her.

She could see and be with her kids before she went to her final resting place. Lord knows that her children were the most important thing to her, so she was allowed to spend her last days on earth with them. The only reason that I was not there due to my incarceration was another sign. The reason that I was not there represents the missing piece to the puzzle that has to be filled to complete my mother's dreams.

Lately I have been trying not to be sad when I think of her. At times I smile because God blessed me with the best mother that He chose for me.

I am her son, still trying to be a man

because on this earth we are far from

being the true men that God created

us to be. The very women that we

neglected and took for granted was

our teacher. She was the womb that

bore us. Now we must do our part and

raise our families right with the love

and care that our mother gave us. In

her last days she stayed true to the

promised that she made to us. She had

surgery two months before she passed

away and they removed her hip in an

attempt to cut away the cancer that

was rapidly spreading throughout her bones. Her condition began to get worse every day, but she fought it until the very end like the warrior that she was. On the outside looking in, you could not tell that the cancer was eating her up because she still looked like her beautiful self. But the pain on the inside was becoming unbearable and everyone who was close to her witnessed this. The whole entire family was there for her. I was told that she smiled everyday bearing the pain and she would joyfully greet each visitor as they came to see her.

Nothing was going to extinguish her determination to win this battle for her life. The doctors continued to run x-rays to see where the cancer was coming from, but they were having a difficult time locating the exact source. My mother was not very fond of hospitals so the majority of the time she stayed at home dealing with the unbearable pain until God decided to release her of that burden. Problems still plagued our household and her illness was not enough to straighten various family members up, so she also had the burden of worrying about their future as well as mine.

I recall our very last conversation about five or so days before she died. It was a short conversation, but I was calling home to check up on her telling her to go to the hospital. Her condition had worsened to the point that she had lost her appetite. She was getting blood clots in her leg causing it to swell up. Her lungs were full of fluid as well because she had lung cancer and another form of cancer. This time when I called, she had finally gone to the hospital so this could only mean that her condition had really worsened. All of my siblings were there, and we were all on the phone. That was the last conversation that my mother had with all of her kids together. My brothers and sister were in the background getting loud about something and I said, "Mama you hear your kids?" She answered in the affirmative. She had been given medication to induce sleep, but she kept fighting her sleep for fear that she would not wake up. When they had went to the hospital, they instantly hooked her up to a breathing machine to help her breathe. She was losing her breath, but she never told anyone in the family because she said she did not want to worry anyone. She was that caring and unselfish that she put everyone else before herself.

Her last words were said to my brothers and sister. The doctors told her that she had a few months to live, then that changed to having only a few days to live. The doctors asked if she wanted to be hooked up to a machine that would leave her in a vegetative state. My mother refused and said that she would rather remain fully conscious and fight her illness until the end. Her lungs kept contracting fluid and making it difficult for her to breathe. The fluid kept spreading so fast that the doctors had to keep puncturing her lungs to get the fluid out and they could no longer do this. They said she only had a few more hours to live. During her last few hours on this earth, she remained her regular self. She stayed up all night and my siblings stayed up with her because the doctors said she may not wake up after she falls asleep. She fought her sleep for a few days while dozing off here and there. I was told that she was waiting on me to call. The night before she died, she stayed up talking to her daughter. Shawn arrived at the hospital and began to cry, but she told him not to cry. She told him that this world is cruel so be careful out there. She had always said that she was going home on a Sunday. She so fought with all of her life that Saturday night until the next morning. The doctors told the family that she was an extraordinarily strong woman. Surrounded by her entire family, including her mother, sisters, nieces, nephews, distant family and friends, she passed away at 12:50 p.m. on December 17, 2000.

ESSAY ONE: "DEAR CHILD"

Dear Child,

This is an essay dedicated to all of the rebellious children of this generation and the up and coming generations. I am one of you, so I write this for you. I know how you feel and how your relationship with your parents affects you. As a child who has learned the hard way through experience, I explain to you the value of a mother. No matter how it seems like she wants to control your life or may be in your business, she only has your best interest at heart.

For many years I have been a hardheaded child and would not listen to anyone. Then when I lost my mother last year to cancer, I realize how important she is to me. I am now 22 years of age and I wrote this essay to you because your mother is probably still alive today and I want to emphasize to you how much you should begin to appreciate her. It took for me to come to prison to understand the unconditional love that my mother had for me. Then when I lost her, there has not been a day that has gone by that I do not wish that I had listened to her when she was here. I wish that I would have showed her how much I love her.

Some people are lucky to have their mother around. So dear child of the present generation, I write this message for you. Please take heed to these words. I write these to ease my conscience and to help you avoid the turmoil that my soul is going through. I remember my mother used to tell me, "You only get one mama." Now all of her sayings and teachings ring true every minute of my life and even though she is physically gone, I find myself talking to her spirit, but wish that I could talk to her. I cannot; now I listen to her, but I did not listen to her when she was here. Imagine the changes that I go through when I see other people with their mother and knowing that mines is gone. Maybe she would still be here if I had not taken her through so much stress. She probably would have lived longer if she did not smoke cigarettes so much because she had to worry about me and my siblings. Every day she was living and breathing she sacrificed her life for us again and again. In turn, we caused her pain and stress. I took her for granted too many times in life and now I am missing her just like she told me I would. This is my testimony to you so that you will know that my words to you are from you. These words that I am writing is the better part of your conscience telling you the consequences of the future and to love and obey your mother as well as appreciating her the way that you should. Some of us never knew or had

our biological mother to raise us, but

even if you had a foster mother, step-

mother, grandmother, auntie, friend,

or sister that played the role as your

mother, you should love her and give

her the same acknowledgement as a

mother because she has been the

mother that you have known.

Dear child, how come when our

mothers tell us something, we do not

listen? Why when our mothers are

telling us something right, we rebel

and do the opposite of what she told

us to do? Why do we always want to

run the streets and worry our mothers? Why when we see the hurt in her eyes, we continue living the lifestyles that we do? Why are we so rebellious? Why do we so often take our mothers for granted? Why do we cause the person that loves us more than anything, so much pain? Why can't we see the things we are taking her through? Why is it hard for us to see that she only wants what is best for us? Why is it that when she worries about our well-being and decide to check up on us, we call it being nosy? Why is it that when she shows concern for our affairs, we automatically assume that she is in our business? Why can't we see the flip side of this? Why is it that when our mothers give us some good advice, we tell her to quit trying to run our lives? The very life that she helped give us. Why do we talk back to our mothers? Why do we whisper smart remarks under our breath when she makes a simple request of us? Why can't we realize that she has feelings and we hurt them every day by our actions and inaction? Why is it that we make it seem so hard to follow her simple rules? Why can't we see all of the sacrifices that she makes for us? All these whys and many more run through our mother's minds everyday as they try to figure out their rebellious children. They tried their best to understand us, but we shut them out because we say that they don't know what they are talking about. The truth is that we are the ones that don't know what we are talking about and we need to open our ears and listen since we are so good at hearing what we want to hear through our music. We want to make it seem as if everything else is the problem when in reality we contribute significantly to the problem without acknowledging it. Now it is time for this generation to look at this thing from its true perspective. Come on and let's quit fooling ourselves. Let us take a good look at our rebellious selves.

The sooner we realize the value of our mother's and begin to treat them the way we are supposed to treat them, the better our lives will become instantly and begin to understand why our mother's do the things they do.

She does these things out of love and care for her children. Here she is the woman that gave us birth and loves us more than anything. Here we are with a sense of rebellion towards her. Some of us have multiple excuses as to why we act the way that we do towards our mothers. Some of them may have boyfriends or husbands that we think they put before us. Some of our mothers are very strict. Some of them we may think are mean. Some of our mothers are too old fashioned in our eyes. They want us to be too much like them, etc., etc. Regardless of all of this, she is still our mother

and some of our views of them are

over exaggerated. We sometimes

develop opinions of our parents from

childish emotions that are rooted in

rebellion that we developed early in

our childhood. All of these baseless

complaints that we have made against

our parents are a result of us wanting

to see things our way. Even the few

legitimate complaints that we make

against our mothers are one sided. We

do not know our mother's intentions

or the reasons that she does what she

does; we automatically assume the

worst of her intentions. So, we rebel

against her advice and we reap the

consequences. So, I ask who is

wrong? Our parents or us? I realize

that our mothers are not perfect.

Think of all of the times that we were

in trouble and she was there for us.

Think of all the times that she was

worried sick about us when we

missed curfew or some other time she

was uncertain of our safety. Think of

all of the sacrifices, the labor, and

care that she has reaped for us.

For many years, we continued

to rebel against our mothers but along

the way she tried to discipline us the best way she could. She provided for us with all the means at her disposal. Some of us were poor but our mother did the best that she could raising us. It would take many sacrifices to talk about all of the sacrifices that our mothers made for us and all the things that they go through on our behalf. We are forever in debt to our mothers.

So, in my conclusion to this essay, I want to talk about how we need to start appreciating our mothers and showing them in our deeds how much we love them. I know that sometimes we may not understand our mother and her intentions, but we need to start listening to them and obeying them. Let's make peace with our mothers. Because if she passes away, we will wish we had done all of these things while she was here. You will only get one mother. I am sharing this advice with you and voicing my opinion with you on this subject because I want to save you from all of the regret and sorrow that I go through because my mother is no longer here for me to show her how much I appreciate her. I now do my best to obey her rules, but she is not here for me to see her smile when I succeed in life by doing what she taught me to do. So, if you do not want to go through these sorts of regrets, please appreciate your mother. Listen to her and show how much you love her. Make your mother proud and happy, listen to her wise words, DEAR CHILD.

ESSAY TWO: "DEAR MOTHER"

Dear Mother,

This is an essay dedicated to every mother of today and yesterday that constantly and continuously make sacrifices and undergo much pain on account of raising and loving their children. Yes, mothers of the world today, if you are reading these words, I want you to know that we your children do love you. We appreciate all that you have done for us even though we have strange ways of showing you. We are sorry mama. When we get into situations we then come to see and realize the value of you. No sooner than we get relieved from the trouble that we are in, we proceed to take on our old rebellious ways. Mother, I know we children are wrong for the disobedience that we show you, but we ask you to please forgive us. I know that we get in trouble and take you through what we take you through. It may appear that we do not care that we are hurting you, but we care. It's just that we are not paying attention to what we are doing. As you already know, we are hurting ourselves more than we are hurting anyone. So, I know that it may appear that we do not even care about ourselves, but we do. We are just unconscious of our actions and bringing the mentality that we learned from the streets into our home.

We just want you to try and understand your children like we want to understand you. We know that we are wrong, so now we want to meet you halfway and show you that we love and appreciate you mother. No one in this world can take your place. We are in great debt to you and we know that there is no way that we can ever pay you back.

All of your years of goodness and kindness towards us is something that we now recognize. We are beginning to see clearly that you are our best friend. Sometimes our stubbornness causes us not to tell you that you were right when you warned us that this or that would happen if we didn't listen to the advice you gave us. Even after this, we somehow wanted to prove you wrong and show that you were old fashioned and did not know what you were talking about. Well at least that is what we thought. When we take that fall that you warned us against, we get up and dust ourselves off and do not even tell you sorry for not listening. Again, and again we take the same falls as a result of not listening to you. We are sorry for hurting you. Really there is no excuse for our actions, but I must try to explain our point of view as your children so that you can begin to understand us a little better. Okay mama, we first started by telling you that we know that we are wrong. We are overcoming denial and admitting our wrong doings, but we want to talk to you today mama. Here goes our point of view so you can understand why we as your kids do things that we do. No matter how rebellious we may be at times, we still love you.

This essay still speaks for all of us kids of this generation. This is because this writing even speaks for the better side of all of our siblings who persist in this rebellion towards millions of mothers in the world today. We are them and they are us so now that we are beginning to realize our value and importance mama, we are trying to reach them just as you have tried to reach us all of our lives. Hopefully all us children wake up one day and start showing you that we really do care mother.

Before we sign off though we must explain a few more things to you mother. All of the countless nights that you could not sleep when we did not come home, we did not even mean to cause you grief, nor stress you out. We were safe having fun with our peers. We dislike for you to

worry so much about us. One thing

that we cannot control is your

worrying because sometimes you

worry too much even when you

yourself know that some

circumstances do not warrant your

extreme worry. To a certain extent

you worry too much and cause

yourself unnecessary grief.

Sometimes we do get careless and we

are sorry mama for all the days and

nights that you spend worrying about

us. Now that we are maturing a little,

we realize what we take you through

and again we are sorry. Dear mama, we appreciate you. There is no way that we can repay you. No words can express our gratitude to you.

Those good visions that you visualized for my future will be something that I will try to fulfill. The potential and greatness that you see in me is something that I will begin to try and tap in to. All the flaws and faults that you have pointed out about my personality, I will begin to try and correct.

Your special day is not only on your birthday or even a holiday. Your day is everyday mama because every day that I live is because you gave birth to me. You are due thanks and we are saying thank you today and forever. We thank you for giving us birth. Thanks for putting your life on the line when you gave us birth and many times after that. Thanks for all the care, love, and affection that you continue to give us. Thank you for loving us more than anyone else in the world and carrying all of the burdens that we put on your back all of these years. We can never thank you enough for all of the good that you have done for us since we were born.

So, we want you to know that we love

you, care for you, and appreciate you.

Mother's Day is every day and

hopefully we will show this more. We

will not be perfect, and we know that

you do not expect us to. This is

written and lived in the ink of our

hearts and DEAR MAMA.

MOTHER'S DAY IS EVERYDAY

Mother's Day is everyday
That's the way it should stay
You are worthy of your children's praise
Happy Mother's Day should be an everyday
phrase
Mama you deserve presents and recognition
more than one day of the year
Throughout all the years of raising me you
always stayed sincere
You are always there for me when no one seems
to care
When I need you, you never forsake me, you
are always there
Even when I am wrong you take my side
If my life was at stake you would always ride
You have given our own life just to protect
mine

The least I can do is devote my time

Mama your day is every day, not just

something to celebrate annually

Without you there would be no me

No one on this earth will ever love me the way

you do

So, no matter how old I get I will always be

your Poo

I can never repay you for all the sacrifices that

you have had to endure

Just to make sure I was happy you had to be

sure

You always took extreme cautions to make sure

that I was safe

You deserve to be cherished for more than one

day

For all of the days that I did not listen you

remained patient

You carried the haven burdens that I left

you to fear when I was an adolescent

So when the holiday called Mother's Day

swing around the way

I'll be sure to tell you mama, that Mother's

Day is everyday

Family Photos

Family Photos

Family Photos

ESSAY THREE: "ADVICE I WOULD GIVE TO MY YOUNGER SELF"

As I sit back and meditate on the many mistakes that I have made in life, I contemplate on the advice that I would give to my younger self. Then again, I wonder would he listen. My 14, 15, or 16-year-old self, thought he had it all figured out. He rebelled against adults because in his young mind, they didn't know what they were talking about. How could they since they couldn't see the world through his eyes. Ironically, now that I am older, I see things differently.

When we are young, we somehow put it in our minds that we will be young forever. How could we ever imagine that we would become those same adults that we rebelled against as we try to give positive advice to our own kids? I never lost touch with my youth; therefore, I understand where that rebellion comes from. Yet my thinking has changed.

At 14, 15, and 16 years old, I saw the world in the way that I wanted to see it. Back then it was only about what I wanted. That included girls, the latest fashions, cars, gangbanging and money. I didn't have a clue about the future, nor did I even care. Why? Because I never thought I would live to be 18 years old. All around me, my peers were getting killed, so it was just a matter of time before I would be next.

My mind was so closed back then. What was I thinking? The problem is that I wasn't thinking. Foolishly, without any rational basis I thought I knew it all. I would make dumb mistake after mistake every day and not really give it a second thought. In my mind, my parents and other nosey adults did not know what they were talking about when they tried to give me positive advice regarding the decisions that I should be making in life. How could they understand me when they had not experienced what I have been through? Besides, this is not the 1970's or 1980's anymore.

Yeah, that little hardheaded fool that I was thought he had it all figured out. So, what advice would I give him today? First, I would have to put myself in his shoes so I could relate to his thinking. Now I realize his thinking was distorted. Ground zero would be that he should listen to his mother. That is common sense; but when you are in your teenage rebellion it is not so logical. After all this time I have learned that it was my mother who was there to rescue me every time that I got into trouble. She was the one who cried because I wouldn't listen to her. I would do the very thing that she would warn me not to do. When my rebellion landed me in serious trouble, she never gloated over my misfortune. On the contrary, she was in pain with me, as well as, for me. When I rebelled against her advice and landed in trouble she never once said: "I told you so." Instead, she was there every time I needed her, unlike my peers.

As a rebellious teenager it was always those same adults who tried to help me when I failed. I would tell my younger self to listen to my mother first of all. She loved you more than anyone else in this world. I would tell my teenage self to "slow down." I would let him know that every decision that you make today will affect your quality of life tomorrow. Once these decisions are made you cannot change them; therefore, you must give serious thought to what you are doing. The world doesn't owe you anything.

Don't spend all your time playing because this will cause you to have to work harder in the long run. Look at the bigger picture and don't just see what is right in front of you. Education doesn't seem all that important to you right now, but it is the foundation stone of everything that you are after. This is the basics of life; you cannot skip over the basics to get into the luxuries of life. When you make mistakes, take time out to evaluate how and why you made this mistake. Catch it before it becomes too big and irreversible. When someone asked you why you made that mistake, you often say:

"I was not thinking." Well younger self, you need to start thinking.

I would again tell my younger self to take responsibility for what you do and stop blaming people for your blunders. I would ask my younger self where do you want to be 5 years from now? What steps are you taking to get there? You have to have a plan and work that plan. As the old saying goes, "If you fail to plan, then you plan to fail." I know that you do not want to fail in life. You want to be successful. Crime is not the way to do that. First, you have to learn what real success is. Right now, your definition of success is distorted.

Study the greats in history that came before you and see how they found success from the ground up. Look to positive inspirational mentors. Even if your reality is hard, look to the future to see how it can one day become better. Work towards that. Do not try to escape reality through drugs and alcohol. Find creative ways to deal with your pain, anger, and frustration. If you are misunderstood, do not feel alienated. Just be who you are and accept yourself for who you are even if others don't. Face reality no matter how difficult it is. Try to change it. You are not helpless to make change in the world. You are not powerless. Do not just see what is wrong with the world and complain about it. See what you can try to do along with others to make the world a better place. Do not be selfish, it is always bigger than just you. Stay grounded and humble. If you do not like the bully, then never become like that person. Do not make your choices strictly from peer pressure. The advice I would keep on giving to younger self is endless, but basically this sums it up. If you are a young teenager, please listen to me. My life is real. What happened to me at 16 years old is real. Read my story and make better decisions than I did.

<u>*Postscript*</u>

Bobby has continued his struggle to become free. He has obtained his Associates of Science degree, completed numerous rehabilitation classes, started a book club and started a non-profit to help troubled teens. The judge who sentenced him has joined the legal fight to help him achieve freedom.

Afterword

It has been 20 years since my mother passed away. Not a day goes by that I don't think about her. When I look at my own flesh, I know that I am alive because she gave birth to me. Her spirit lives on. I believe that the contents of this book are timeless. Although it is a book about her life, it is a tribute to every single mother and all mothers in general. It is also a book of lessons to us children of single mothers. When my mother died on December 17, 2000, I mourned for several days and then I decided to write this book as a memorial to her. Within three months, this book was complete.

I typed up the manuscript and then sent it home. I wanted to publish this book many years ago. It set dormant in my sister's closet until she shared it with a co-worker who was so moved by the story that she convinced my sister this book was so important that it needed to be published immediately. From that conversation, you now hold this book in your hands.

Mothers seem to have a God given intuition to prophesize things in their children's future. They know their children like a well-studied book. Our mother's see our gifts and talents even before we have an inkling of what we want to do with our lives. Often, we rebel against them to our own peril. My mother could see years ahead into my future. She knew that I was book smart. But I wonder did she ever know that I would be the first one in our family to graduate college. How could she know? All I know is that God must have told her so.

A lot has taken place in the two decades that my mother passed away. Yet, the mother/child relationship that me and she shared, plays out everyday with hundreds of thousands of mothers and sons/daughters. That is why the contents of our story in this book are timeless. I will not go off into depth of all of the things that have taken place in my life and my family's life since she passed away. For more on my life story, see my autobiography, "Humbled to The Dust: Still I Rise" which will be released soon or could already be in the bookstores by the time you read this. For more general information on me and my journey, Google my name: Bobby Bostic.

I do want to share a few brief details with the readers. My sister Keeda had two more children after my mother passed away. Her daughter, Marshaun Bostic, is a teenager who is a rising basketball star. Her son, Marzell, is a teenager who plays football. Sadly, in May 2006, my brother

Shawn died at 26 years old due to health complications. As for my own journey for freedom, the United States Supreme Court has come out with several decisions prohibiting juveniles (anyone under 18 years old when they committed their crime) from being sentenced to life without parole. My sentence of 241 years amounts to life with no chance of parole in my lifetime. A slew of legal activity has taken place to get me released from prison. The judge who sentenced me to die in prison has come forth to help me get out of prison. She now regrets giving me such a harsh sentence for a crime in which no one was seriously injured. In fact, she came to this prison to visit me and talk to me about my journey in prison as well as the changes and accomplishments that I have achieved despite my situation.

In 2020, I got an Associates of Science degree from Adams State University. I am not working on my bachelor's degree in Social Work. I plan on starting my own publishing company with the 15 books that I have written since I have been in prison. My other ultimate goal is to give back to kids by starting non-profits to keep kids out of trouble. I want to use my story to deter them from making the terrible mistakes that I made at such a young age.

But this story is not about me. My story has been written elsewhere. I just want mothers to know that in time, your troubled kids can learn to find their way. Please don't give up on them. The potential that you see in your kids is real. In their rebellion, they don't care. Give them time to find themselves. They may have to learn the hard way. That is just the trials that people have to go through. It would be much easier if they take the path that you are trying to guide them on. Just as the baby boomers before us, we often rebel against our parents and have to bump our heads against the wall. In our youth, we think that they are out of touch with the times or that they do not know what they are talking about. In the long run, we realize that they were right.

So, for every mother dealing with a rebellious youth, please remain vigilant as well as patient with your children. My advice to the rebellious youth is that you should listen to your parents. Please don't learn the hard way like I had to. Nine times out of ten, your parents are right. They have your best interest at heart. Listening to them will only benefit you. Mama, I wish I would have listened to you. You sure knew what you were talking about. My mother was not perfect, and she made many mistakes. But to me, she is the greatest mother. She taught me so many things. My mother even taught us what no to do by the many mistakes that she made. This is why I think that my sister has turned out to be such a great parent. She raised her children so successfully well because she learned from our mother's mistakes in raising us. She took the good and the bad of our childhood, which allowed her to give her kids a better childhood. Her kids do not live in abject poverty that we lived in. They are not involved in criminal activities. The cycle can be broken.

Us kids must not hold our parents to such a high standard. We must understand that they are humans too and will make mistakes. But please listen to them. Our parents love us. They will not be here forever. Please enjoy the time that you have with them. They cannot be replaced. Appreciate your parents while they are living because when they leave this world, that time can never be given back. Love them for who they are; flaws and all. Learn from my story. Please take this book to heart. Feel what was written. Use your own life experience as a roadmap. "Dear Mama" was written for everybody. I dedicate this book to every hard-working single mother out there. Your worth cannot be summed up in words. You are timeless. All of the hard work and sacrifices that you make for us seem to go unnoticed. But your blood, sweat and tears are not in vain. You are doing a good job, but we seem to go out of our way to make your job even harder as a mother. We admire you even though we don't know how to tell you. To all the mothers, we your children love you. Please forgive us. Forgive us for all the heartache we cause you, all the pain, and all the worry. To every mother, forgive us. From the deepest part of our hearts we speak these truths to you "Dear

Mama."

WE LOVE YOU MAMA

Other Books by Bobby Bostic

Time

Endless Moments

In Prison

Generation
Misunderstood:
Generation Next

Mind Diamonds:
Shining on Your
Mind

Mental Jewelry:
Wear It on Your
Brain

When Life Gives
You lemons:
Make Lemonade

Life Goes On

Inside Prison

Also look for future books, products,

and merchandise by Bobby Bostic.

Made in the USA
Columbia, SC
26 November 2022